# Jackie Bushman's Big Buck Strategies

# Jackie Bushman's Big Buck Strategies

## Tactics and Keys To Success

## By Jackie Bushman

The Lyons Press

Guilford, Connecticut

An imprint of The Globe Pequot Press

The Lyons Press is an imprint of the Globe Pequot Press.

Printed in the United States of America

Designed by Compset, Inc.

10 9 8 7 6 5 4 3 2 1

Library of Congress Cataloging-in-Publication Data is available on file.

# Acknowledgments

My sincere thanks to Buckmasters artists Tim Martin, Laura Unger, and John Manfredi for illustrating the set-ups for the hunts in this book on relatively short notice with their usual professionalism and dedication to detail.

Thanks to Gene Bidlespacher, who took most of the photos in this book, and to these photographers who took the remainder: Elliott Allen, Alan Brewer, Neil Courtice, Tim Craig, Pat Gregory, John Harrell, Russ Thornberry, George Warner.

The artists and photographers gave this book the extra spark it needed.

Jackie with Gene Bidlespacher

# Dedication

This book is dedicated to the Buckmasters TV series crews who have made the series and our video tapes such a success over the years.

Dan Black Productions did our first shows back in the late 1980s. Dan had helped me produce my first video, a two-hour instructional tape titled "The Basics of Hunting the Whitetail Buck." The success of that tape helped launch Buckmasters.

After that, Dan helped us produce the pilot for our show on TNN. It aired in 1988. Representatives of TNN were so impressed that they flew to Montgomery the next day to negotiate what was to become the Buckmasters TV series. It was a significant meeting in that it was the first hunting series on TNN and the first deer hunting series on network TV.

We later brought production of the series in-house. Pat Gregory, our next producer, set up a studio in our building and traveled all across the country with me taping the shows. We had a great run with both Dan and Pat and appreciate their efforts.

Today, we're fortunate to have one of the best whitetail men in the business, Gene Bidlespacher, leading our video team. Before joining Buckmasters, Gene headed up his own company, Whitetail Visions, and produced some of the best action-packed "How-To" video tapes in the business. His "October Whitetails" became one of the most recognized deer hunting tapes in the country.

Gene came to work with us in the fall of 1993. For many years, it was just the two of us on the road with a camera. His dedication to Buckmasters and his professionalism have been invaluable to our TV series and the Buckmasters video tapes which have entertained millions of people over the years.

Mark Oliver joined the crew as a videographer in 1995. Mark does a great job. He was excited about the opportunity and his eagerness propelled him to the position of editor of the series in just two short years.

Elliott Allen, another of our videographers, has been with Buckmasters since Day 1. Elliott and I have hunted together for many, many years. Elliot can do anything and he's probably the hardest worker of any of us here at Buckmasters. He has a special talent for putting up tree stands. I tell people that he's the best tree-stand-putter-upper in the country.

Jimmy Little serves in dual roles of videographer and also a valued member of our advertising sales team. Jimmy's doing a great job in both areas. Like the other members of the crew, Jimmy is an avid outdoorsman and the move to TV is one he picked up naturally.

The Buckmasters TV crew puts in endless hours of hard work to get the show on the air each week. That's a lot harder than it looks. In addition to videoing, they also put up tree stands, get the set-ups right, work with the sponsors and a lot more. Their days are long and hard and often cold and uncomfortable. We start the end of August and go all the way through the end of January taping shows during hunting season and then they sit down and log the miles of footage; write the scripts; and edit the tape.

These guys behind the scenes are the ones that make it happen. I'm grateful to them and really proud of them and what they've done. This book is dedicated to them.

# Contents

CONTENTS

# 1

# The Drop-Tine Buck

**O**ur Buckmasters crew had hunted the same place in Alberta, Canada, off and on for 10 years. We'd taken some good bucks there, but the rancher kept telling us about this monster drop-tine buck. That deer became a vision that I couldn't get out of my mind, like a kid fantasizing about Christmas morning.

We went to Alberta for opening day, 1998. It was warm with a full moon. As we were walking to the stand before daylight, I spotted something white beside the trail. We weren't 200 yards from the house. It was a shed antler from the drop-tine buck. I told my producer, Gene Bidlespacher, that "this could be an omen."

The hunting was slow and we didn't see much, so we flew back home after a few days, and returned the next week. The weather was a little colder the second week and we saw some pretty good bucks, including a heavy 10-pointer that made

1

me take the safety off, only to decide that we could find a bigger buck. And let me tell you, it's tough letting an outstanding buck walk, even if you do know that there are bigger ones around.

I usually go with my gut feeling, and it's been wrong a few times. This time, my gut feeling was right. We were about to climb down from the tree stand when we saw the rancher's truck coming. He drove right under the stand, and told us he had seen a big buck bedded in a nearby field.

We drove over to look at the deer. He was with three does way out in the middle of a huge field. Gene and I got below the hill and crawled up to a fence that was covered with sage. At 800 yards, with my naked eye, the buck's antlers looked like goal posts out in that field. When you see a really big buck, it looks like a cartoon character. The rack is disproportionate to the body. When I looked at him through my binoculars, I saw the drop as clear as day. I was shaking from excitement. This was the deer I'd been dreaming about, and he was, from vantage point, bedded in what seemed to be an impossible place. We had the thick cover behind us, and that's the only advantage we had.

2

We sat out there awhile until a ranch truck came down the road on the other side of the deer. To our surprise, they got up and came our way. I calmed myself down by not looking at the buck's antlers and by telling myself it was just another deer. Negative thoughts produce negative results, and I wanted this deer.

The does veered off, but the buck headed toward the woods. He crossed the fence below us. There was a dike between me and the buck, and all I could see was the top of his back. Then he came up on the dike, angling toward us a little. When he got as close as I thought he was going to get, I grunted and he stopped. He didn't stop for long, and I shot just as he started moving again. I hit him, but he took off running. I fired a second shot and had no idea where it hit. The deer stopped again, and I put him down with a third shot. Later, we determined that the first shot would have done the trick.

I've been doing television for more than 15 years, but I was speechless when I walked up on that deer. He was such a

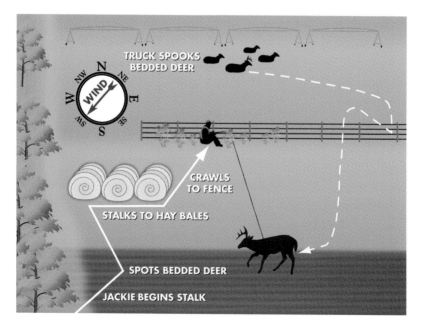

magnificent animal. He had 191 inches of antler, 15 points, 26 inches of spread. His drop tine was more than nine inches long. It was an unforgettable experience.

# TACTICAL BREAKDOWN

You're unlikely to shoot a really big buck if you're willing to settle for something less. That was an important point for the drop-tine buck, because I passed up an outstanding buck that same morning.

When we saw the buck, we had cover behind us. We would have been in trouble without that cover. When deer are exposed in an open place like that and they get nervous, they're usually going to head to the woods or thick brush. We were patient until the deer came our way. Knowing when to shoot is also critical. I used a rangefinder to range a fencepost that was 300 yards away, and I also ranged the dike. When the buck came up on the dike, I knew he was close enough to shoot.

I didn't have a bipod with me because I'd been hunting in a tree stand. Still, I was able to get a solid rest by sitting with my back to a fencepost. I put my backpack in my lap, rested my rifle on the pack, and steadied my elbow on my knee.

## Keys to Success

- Be willing to pass up a good buck and hold out for a great buck.
- Hunt during the rut, when mature bucks are more likely to make a mistake.
- Know the habits of deer. Whitetails in an exposed place will head for the nearest cover if spooked.
- Know when to take the shot and how to get a solid rest.

# 2

# Consolation Prize

We traveled from what had been a slow hunt in Illinois to Iowa, where our country music friend John Anderson was hosting a celebrity hunt. We were going to hunt on property owned by Tony Knight, who makes Knight Muzzleloaders. It had been unusually hot in Illinois, and we didn't know what to expect in Iowa. We got to our motel and checked in after midnight.

When the alarm went off at 5:30 a.m., I looked outside the window and was astonished to see that it was snowing so hard I couldn't see the cars in the parking lot. We slept in. It's been my experience that when you have a big snowfall, it takes the deer at least 24 hours to recover and start moving.

We hunted that afternoon and didn't see much. The next morning, Tony put us in a stand that he called his center stand. It

was a good location, and Tony had seen two big bucks in the area. The deer started moving in the afternoon. About 4:00 p.m., I saw some does and then another deer walking through the woods. The deer stopped behind some trees, and I could see its face but no antlers. He looked like a buck. When the deer stepped out from behind the trees, I realized I was looking at the biggest buck I'd ever seen! This deer, a 10-pointer, easily had 200 inches of antler!

Tony had set up the blinds, with Gene Bidlespacher's camera blind directly behind mine. When we set up our own blinds, we usually put the camera blind higher. I was hunting with a muzzleloader, and I got a solid rest on my stand. The deer walked out in the open and I was rock solid on him, but the camera was right behind me and Gene motioned that he couldn't get the deer on camera. The monster buck stood there 10 seconds, then walked over behind some trees and started making a scrape. We watched him through the trees for 30 minutes. To see a deer of that caliber is incredible. Everybody tells me I should have shot the buck, but shooting a buck for my personal benefit is not my job. I felt we still had a chance to get that buck on video.

The next morning, we went back to the center stand. About 9:00 a.m., Gene saw a buck chasing a doe on a nearby ridge. Then we saw a bigger buck join in the chase. The deer were across a fence, but I could tell the bigger deer was a good buck, and I was hoping it was the deer we'd seen the previous day.

Luckily, the doe jumped the fence and blew right past our stand. I whispered to Gene to get ready, and here came the big buck! I had twisted around in the stand because the deer were behind us, and I was getting a rest against the tree. The buck jumped over a brushpile that looked like it was 10 feet high, and when he got close he looked like he was all antlers. I was relatively new to muzzleloader hunting, and all I could think was I only had one shot.

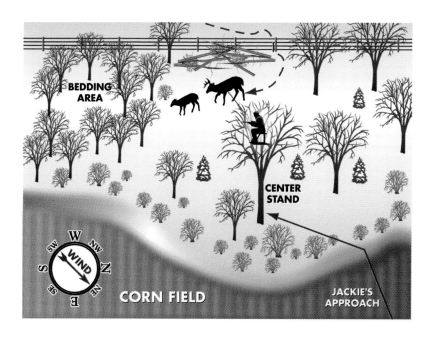

I got the safety off and found the deer in the scope. I grunted, and he whirled and stopped broadside at 20 steps. I let the shot go and there was smoke everywhere, but I could tell by the way the buck ran that he was hit hard. He was a tremendous buck, the smaller of the two bucks we'd been hunting, but what a consolation prize! Even with a broken brow tine, he had 171 inches of antler.

# TACTICAL BREAKDOWN

We had a weather change that triggered the rut and a burst of deer movement. The hunting had been slow until the weather turned cold. Though the stand setup was not ideal for video, the location was excellent. We were surrounded by bedding areas, and the wind was perfect.

I was able to improvise a solid rifle rest in my stand, and I grunted to stop a moving deer. I concentrated on keeping my head down and my eye in the scope when I shot. There's a tiny delay with a muzzleloader, and you have to hang in there until the powder explodes.

## Keys to Success

- Pay attention to weather changes that trigger the rut and an increase of deer activity.
- Use the wind to your advantage.
- Pick your stand carefully, and listen to local experts.
- Concentrate on making one shot count with a muzzleloader.

# 3

# The Off-Camera Buck

When I first saw Ron Doering's The Hunt Club in southern Illinois, it didn't look like great whitetail habitat. One morning hunt was all it took to change my mind. Ron has 18,000 acres that he manages by planting soybeans, alfalfa, and corn for the deer to eat. This area of Illinois is mined for coal, and the soil has a lot of minerals that help the deer grow oversized racks. There are some 200-inch deer in those woods. The other thing Ron does is let the bucks mature enough to develop into trophies. Of course, Illinois also has a short firearms season, for shotguns only.

I was hunting opening day of the shotgun season, and Ron put Gene Bidlespacher and me in a stand on a ridge where we could see across a clear-cut. We'd be hunting the edges of that cleared area. The woods around us were extremely thick. I used

the rangefinder, and realized I wouldn't have a shot longer than 90 yards, which was fine with me. My slug gun shoots a two-inch group at 100 yards, but I don't like to shoot any farther than that.

The woods near our stand were full of scrapes and sign. It was a warm, foggy, rainy morning, and the moisture was playing havoc with our camera. In fact, it wasn't long after daylight when Gene told me that the camera had shut down. "You know what's about to happen," I said.

It wasn't more than 45 minutes later that I saw a doe crossing an open lane in front of us. A buck was following right behind her. Ron wanted me to take a good buck so we could get a story for the magazine. The first thing I noticed about the buck was his gnarly bases, and when you see that, you're usually looking at a mature buck. The deer had an exceptional spread and a lot of mass, and I whispered to Gene that the buck was a shooter. He reminded me that the camera was shut down, and I told him I was going to take the buck, anyway.

The buck was about to cross an open lane at 25 yards, and I was wishing for a bow. What a deer that would have been to take with a bow! I had a solid rest, and I grunted when the deer stepped out. He stopped and I shot. A shotgun doesn't have as delicate a trigger as a rifle, and I have a tendency to shoot a little high because of the heavier trigger pull. I concentrated on aiming at the lower one-third of the buck's body.

I could tell the deer was hit hard, and I could hear him crashing through the thick cover. We climbed down and went to the last place where we heard the buck, and he was lying right there. Other than determining if he's a shooter or not, I don't really evaluate a deer before I shoot. When I walked up on that

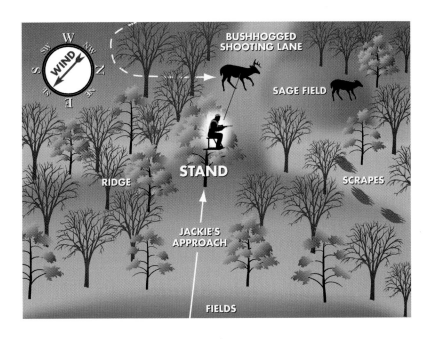

Illinois deer, that was the first real good look I'd taken at his rack and boy was I happy! He was a mainframe 9-pointer with a fork on his right G-2, and he grossed 167 inches. It was extremely disappointing when we couldn't get the deer on video, and that's the only one I've ever shot when I knew we were unable to video.

# TACTICAL BREAKDOWN

You can't take a big buck where they don't exist. Hunting on well-managed property such as The Hunt Club greatly improves your chances of success. Our stand location that morning was in an area of heavy deer activity with lots of fresh sign, including active scrapes.

When you're hunting in tight cover, you have to be able to assess a deer quickly to determine if he's a shooter. You may only have a few seconds to make a shot as the buck crosses an opening, and there's not much time to study the buck before making a decision. Always listen intently when you shoot and the deer runs away. Many times, you'll hear a mortally wounded deer crashing through cover, and you may hear him go down.

## Keys to Success

- To bag a big buck, hunt where those deer are common.
- Pick a stand location where deer activity is high.
- Know what you're looking for and quickly assess whether the buck is a shooter.
- Listen closely when hit deer run away. If there's no blood trail, listening to the deer flee tells you where to start looking.

# 4

# Bruiser Buck With a Bow

There's a great place in Montana that the Buckmasters crew has hunted for years. It's one of the best bowhunting places I've ever seen. The habitat just sets up well for bowhunting. This property has predictable food sources—the farmers grow sugar beets, corn, and alfalfa—and the bedding areas have good bottlenecks between them. The hunting is best in dry years. That's when natural food sources are scarce and deer are forced to come out during daylight to feed on the irrigated crops. They still feed on crops in wet years, but they come to the fields after dark and leave before daylight during such periods.

This particular October, my producer, Gene Bidlespacher, went out to Montana a couple of days early so he could watch how the deer were entering and leaving the fields. We've hunted

that place so often that we know it like the backs of our hands, and we've got six or seven different stand setups that we can use, depending on how the deer are moving. Even on a place that we know so well, scouting is very important. It's a mistake to assume the deer are going to move the same way this year that they moved last year. Deer respond to subtle changes, and there's no substitute for scouting to keep up with their routines.

Gene spotted a couple of good bucks during his scouting and we got out early the first day of the hunt. It was just breaking daylight when I spotted a monster buck coming right toward us. "Get ready, Gene," I whispered, "here comes a shooter." The deer was a huge 10-pointer with extra points around his brow tines. We were still using a Beta-format camera, and Gene didn't have enough light to video.

The buck came closer and closer until he was only 10 yards away, feeding broadside. He was broadside for five minutes, and we still didn't have enough light! He eventually fed out of range by the time we had enough light for video. These days we've switched to digital cameras that will video in very low light conditions, but those old cameras cost us some good bucks. That particular deer would have been my best with a bow.

We hunted that buck for a couple of days and didn't see him again. Then we moved to another stand location where we could see bucks cutting through the cottonwoods. We saw five or six nice bucks that morning, and Gene finally saw a shooter coming from behind us, slightly to our left. Being left-handed, I tried to twist around so I could get a shot. It seems like they

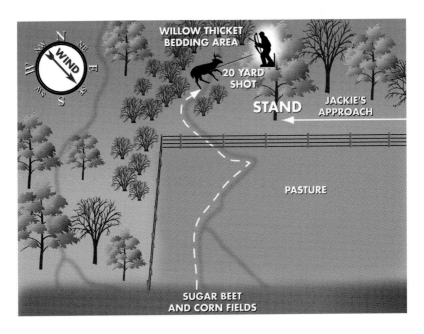

always approach from the wrong side! Fortunately, I was hunting from an API Twister Stand with a swivel seat that makes it easier to move around. The buck finally walked right under the stand and I was able to draw, get on him, and grunt to stop him. I made a good shot and he didn't go far. The buck had 140 inches of antler, and that's a pretty good buck to take with a bow.

As it turns out, *Buckmasters* magazine editor Russell Thornberry eventually got the buck we'd passed up because of poor light the first day. He scored 165, an absolutely incredible buck!

# TACTICAL BREAKDOWN

Scouting is time well spent. Especially when you're bowhunting, just being able to see the deer is not good enough. You've got to set up where you'll have a 30-yard or closer shot when a buck comes by.

You can learn a lot by keeping up with summer weather conditions. Because of the dry summer, we knew deer would be feeding in the irrigated fields during daylight. We also knew how the deer move through the transition areas, and we had several stand setups that we could use to get good shots.

## Keys to Success

- Scout before the hunt.
- Study weather patterns to help identify food sources.
- Hunt a good area repeatedly so you can learn deer movements.
- Have several stand setups to intercept the deer in the areas where they are moving.

# 5

# High-Anxiety Hunt

Idaho is one of the prettiest places I've hunted whitetails, and Tim Craig of Boulder Creek Outfitters is one of the most knowledgeable guides I've hunted with. I got a really good buck with Tim one year, but it was definitely a high-anxiety deer hunt. We were hunting in a series of canyons with extremely brushy bottoms. We had eased up on a point, and I rolled a big rock off into the canyon to see if we could get a deer to move.

A doe and small buck jumped up and took off down the bottom. Along the way, they picked up a good buck. I could see that his rack was very wide (26 inches), and I told Tim it was a shooter. The deer ran up on the far side of the canyon and stopped. They were startled by the rolling rock but not spooked.

They eventually started feeding, so I crawled about 300 yards closer and got a solid rest on a rock.

We'd gotten into camp late the previous night, and going against my normal practice of shooting some practice rounds after traveling, I hadn't had a chance to fire my rifle. I put the crosshairs on that buck, squeezed off, and he never even looked up. I figured it must be farther than I thought, so I held about three inches over his back and shot again. Same result. I fired four shots and then reloaded. By now the deer were moving. The doe was on top of the ridge and the buck was 20 yards below her. I fired again and saw the bullet hit 10 yards to the left of the doe. The deer went over the ridge and I was sick.

In fact, I had such a sick feeling that I wanted to stop hunting and go back to the camp, but Tim wouldn't let me quit. He said we'd find the buck again in the next canyon. My backup rifle was in the truck, so we got it out, loaded up, and went to the other canyon. There were no deer visible, and I could see only four little brush patches along the canyon bottom where deer might be hiding. Tim made a drive around the edge of the first patch of cover and one doe came out. We were moving on to the next patch when I caught a movement behind me. Here came another doe out the backside of the brush, and the big buck was right behind her!

I sat down and got a good rest just as the deer stopped broadside. I squeezed the trigger and the gun clicked. The shell didn't go off! Now the buck started running, so we ran over the top to try and cut him off. He came across an opening about 80 yards away and the rifle misfired again. I jacked another shell in and whistled. The buck stopped, and this time the rifle fired and I got him.

My first rifle was so badly off that it wouldn't hit a paper target at 25 yards. My backup rifle had a dirty firing pin that was

barely striking the cartridge primer. That was my fault. I'll never fly to another deer hunt without firing my rifle at a target before I hunt, even if I have to shoot by truck headlights at night.

# TACTICAL BREAKDOWN

The key to success on this big buck is that I took the local expert's advice. When I missed the buck, Tim Craig knew the deer would move to the next canyon and we'd find him again. Whitetails are similar wherever you find them, but they tend to react differently in different habitat. We also used a hunting technique that I've used at other places—rolling rocks to get the deer moving.

It's important to have a backup gun in case your primary gun develops a problem. Finally, you have to hang in there and keep your confidence. A lot of bad things happened to me on the day, and it looked as if the deck were stacked against me. But I kept putting the crosshairs on that buck until it finally worked.

## Keys to Success

- Take the local experts' advice—they know the deer and the area better than you do.
- Roll or throw a rock to flush deer from their hideout.
- Always carry a backup gun.
- Shoot at a paper target before hunting deer, no matter what.
- Don't lose confidence when things are going bad.

# 6

# Scrapeline Buck

O n one of the trips we made to Idaho, I decided to do something a little different. The previous year, I'd noticed a prominent scrapeline and a bunch of rubs in a canyon. Rather than spot and stalk or rocking the canyons, I decided to hunt that scrapeline. We went in one afternoon and scouted the bottom.

I could tell which way the bucks were moving to the scrapes by the way the leaves were pulled out. We found one scrape in particular that really had a lot of sign in it. When we looked around, we found a perfect vantage point up on the ridge opposite the scrape. When I'm hunting from a tree stand, I like to find what I call the perfect tree. In this case, I found the perfect rock. Not only was this rock a good vantage point where I could see the whole bottom, it was a solid rifle rest when it came time

to shoot. As a left-hander, I've learned to look for a rock where I can sit on the right side and better rest my elbow and rifle. A right-hander does better from the left side of the rock.

Pat Gregory was my cameraman that year and we went to our stand very early the next morning. I didn't want to walk through the bottom and leave scent that might spook the deer, and I didn't want them to see or hear us coming across the top. We walked more than a mile, leaving the truck early enough to get to our stand 45 minutes before daylight. We came over the top in pitch dark and moved slowly to keep the noise to a minimum.

We started seeing deer shortly after daylight—mostly does and a few small bucks. I looked down the draw, though, and here came a shooter! The buck walked back into the brush and worked a scrape. I could see the vines shaking where he was rubbing his face in them. Then he came back our way and disappeared again to work another scrape. Most of the scrapes were in the thickest cover in the bottom of the draw.

The setup was working just as I'd planned, but I hadn't planned on the steep camera angle. Pat had the camera on a tripod and the buck was directly under us at an angle too steep for the camera to get on him. The buck appeared again, then turned and started walking right to us. He was a huge 8-pointer. We didn't realize it at the time, but the deer had a scrape about 100 yards down the slope from our position.

I asked Pat if he could film the deer, and I thought he answered that he could. As it turns out, Pat said that he could

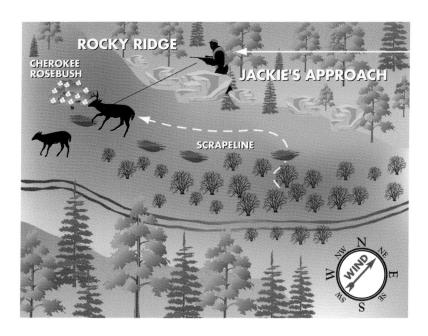

not get on the deer and I misunderstood what he had said. The deer walked up and worked his scrape, then got up on his hind legs and rubbed his face in the brush. When he came down on all fours, he was broadside and I took the shot. I was certain that we were getting great video and we weren't getting any video at all! That was a wonderful 8-pointer with nearly 150 inches of antler.

# TACTICAL BREAKDOWN

I knew the terrain because we'd hunted that area the previous year. I remembered where the scrapeline was. Bucks will usually make scrapes in the same places year after year. Scrape hunting is like working a puzzle. It feels great when the pieces all fit together.

To avoid disturbing the hunting area, we made a long, roundabout walk well before daylight. We also had the wind in our favor. As always, I picked a stand that provided a solid rifle rest. We had rocks all around us and were not on the skyline. It's important to stay below the skyline; otherwise, you're easy to see.

## Keys to Success

- Learn the terrain you're hunting.
- Remember where you see scrapes, because bucks usually make scrapes in the same places year after year.
- Study scrapes to determine how the deer approach them.
- Even if it means a long walk in the dark, approach your stand site so you don't disturb the deer.
- Stay below the skyline in hilly terrain.

# The Woodlot Buck

We were having a very slow hunt in Alberta one fall. Everything was against us: The weather was extremely warm and windy; there was a full moon; and the deer weren't moving during daylight hours. We had some good tree stand setups, but we weren't seeing much.

One afternoon, the rancher whose property we were hunting mentioned he had to go check some cows. Because we knew the land, we knew the rancher would wind up driving alongside a woodlot that deer used for bedding cover. Most of the cover in that area consists of thick woodlots; some are pretty small, but the deer use them a lot. The wind direction was perfect to push the rancher's scent into the woods where we figured some deer would be bedded.

*Credit: Gene Bidlespacher*

We'd hunted that property several times and we knew the deer would come out of the bedding area across a bottleneck and head for the next patch of wood. There was a fairly open sand hill between the two woodlots, so that's where we set up. The wind was blowing to us, and we could hear the rancher's truck coming along the other side of the woodlot. We heard his door slam when he got out to check the cows.

In just a few seconds, we could see deer moving through the thick cover toward us. There were some does and even some mule deer bouncing along in their pogo-stick gait. Then I saw a pretty good buck and I told my producer, Gene Bidlespacher, to get ready with the camera. About that time Gene said "There's a shooter buck!"

I was looking at the deer and said that it was a pretty nice buck, but not a shooter. We got into an argument that was kind of comical. We were looking at two different deer! I finally saw the buck Gene was looking at and he was a whopper. He was also in a hurry to get across the open area and into the next cover. I was lying down on a sand dune, using my backpack for a rifle rest.

The deer was running and I grunted at him and pointed my rifle ahead of him. He was moving so fast that I didn't expect him to stop instantly, but that's exactly what he did. Gene was saying "shoot, shoot," but I couldn't see the deer. I finally eased my head up off the scope and saw the buck standing about 10 feet to the left of where I was looking. I eased the rifle around and got off a shot just as the deer started moving again. I wasn't sure whether I'd hit him or not.

I made a circle to where I thought the deer had gone and found no sign. I was starting to get a sick feeling in the pit of my stomach when Gene whistled and signaled that he'd found the buck. Then he signaled that it was a little one and I felt sick

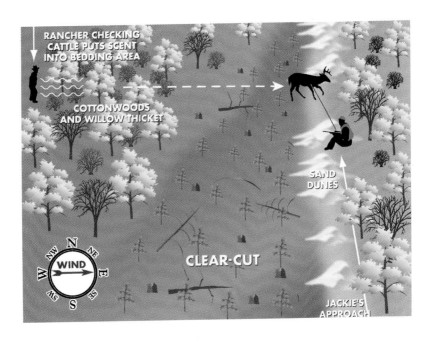

again. Gene likes to fool with me. That buck had 13 scorable points and 170 inches of antler. I'll take a "little one" like that any day!

# TACTICAL BREAKDOWN

When the deer aren't moving, you sometimes have to make something happen. We'd hunted this property enough times to know how the deer move from one clump of cover to the next and we set up in a perfect spot to intercept them. We took advantage of the rancher's normal routine, but you can also stage silent drives like this with your hunting companions.

I was using my backpack for a rifle rest, and both Gene and I recognized the big deer as a shooter as soon as we saw him. When deer are moving, you don't have much time to evaluate them.

## Keys to Success

- Know the country you're hunting and how deer use their escape routes.
- Take advantage of normal farm and ranch activities that may cause deer to move.
- Be prepared to evaluate a buck quickly and make a quick shot.
- If the hunting is slow, make the deer move by staging silent drives.
- If you're trying to stop a running deer, keep your eye on the deer, not on where you expect him to stop.

# 8

# Woodline 8-Pointer

We hunted in Alberta in the fall of 2000 and had good weather. It was cold with plenty of snow—the best conditions you could hope for, because deer really stand out against the snow. The deer were feeding actively because of the cold, and the rut was just starting.

That first morning, we set up on the edge of a huge agricultural field that had 10 willows in a line coming off one corner. We saw a lot of deer in the early morning, including one heavy-horned 9-pointer. He was a good one, but I knew there were bigger deer around. Alberta had had good weather in the spring, and some of the deer had grown exceptional antlers. I passed on the 9-pointer.

The rancher had told us about an exceptional 10-pointer that he had seen, and that's the deer we were looking for. The bucks in that area like to tear up willow bushes, and make their scrapes

under willows, so I kept my eye on that line of willows. Around 11:00 a.m. I looked over at the willows and saw a buck so big that he looked like a bull. When I glassed him, I saw that he was an 8-pointer. He had mass, width, height, everything but 10 points. He was a great 8-pointer, but it was the first morning and I let him go. When we got back at the house, we looked at the video and figured that 8-pointer was close to 160 inches—an incredible deer.

We hunted the next day and saw several more deer. We saw a buck that may have been the big 8, but he was a long way off. The wind shifted late in the morning, so we had to change our stand location to keep the wind in our favor. We improvised by setting up a ground blind, which we got into early that afternoon because the deer were coming into the field by 2:30 p.m. It was extremely cold.

I used my rangefinder to range to the edge of the woods, and determined it was about 200 yards to where the deer were coming out. We'd scouted the edge and knew where the major trails were. It's important to know where the deer are bedding and what trails they're using, but it's *critical* to stay far enough from the bedding areas so you don't spook the deer.

The deer we had observed would come to the edge of the field, stop, and look around to see if there was any danger. They had to cross a 400- or 500-yard opening to reach the peas they were feeding on. Once they committed, they'd run to the feeding area.

It was almost dark when I saw a buck moving through the woods. The deer came right to the edge of the woods and stopped. I could see it was the big 8-pointer. He was standing head on. I had my rifle up, but I don't like to take head-on shots. Some does had passed us earlier, and now one of them came running back by us, stiff-legged and acting spooky. I don't know if she saw us move or caught our wind, but she didn't like it.

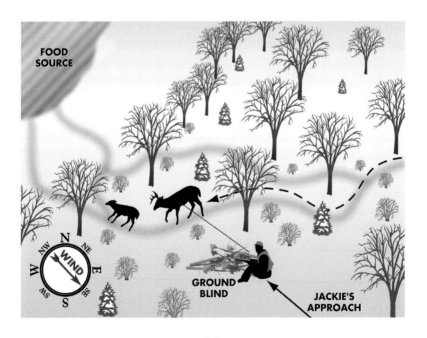

I could see the concern in that buck's eyes as he watched the doe. I saw his muscles tense and I knew he was about to spook. He turned just a bit and I was able to aim at the top of his shoulder and make the shot. If I'd waited a second longer, he would have been gone. I was fortunate. And to be able to walk up on a *300-pound* 8-pointer with 160 inches of antler is an unforgettable experience.

# TACTICAL BREAKDOWN

We had good weather on this hunt and the deer were very active. We knew the food sources they were using and were able to set up and catch the deer moving back and forth between them. When the wind changed, we abandoned our tree stand and improvised by constructing a ground blind so we could stay downwind of the deer.

A big buck is often the last deer to come out, so we had to stay alert all afternoon. Because I could read the 8-pointer's body language, I knew when he was about to spook. I always hope for a perfect, broadside shot, but you sometimes have to take what's available.

## Keys to Success

- Having paid attention to weather patterns all year, we knew Alberta had had a relatively mild winter—we anticipated seeing some good racks.
- We also spoke with the farmer, who clued us in to the big 10-pointer (which we didn't see).
- I passed on a nice 9-pointer, knowing that I would eventually see bigger deer.

# 9

# Early-Season Whitetail

We hunted in northern Alberta one year during a special September season. The weather was perfect—about 50°F during the day. It was great, because I hate being cold. The cottonwood leaves were yellow and the countryside was just beautiful.

We were hunting with Neil Courtice of Big White Outfitters, in an area where the croplands met deep woods—prime deer habitat. Alberta is always an exciting place to hunt because you might see an absolute giant buck at any moment. It can also be slow. We once hunted there for a week and didn't see a buck.

On this particular hunt, the deer were feeding in alfalfa fields and we'd scouted a couple of spots and set up our tree stands. Pat Gregory was my cameraman, and he was in a tree stand right behind mine. We used hand signals to communicate.

Credit: Neil Courtice

On the last afternoon of our hunt, I looked at Pat and saw him making some kind of signal that I didn't understand. I kept shrugging my shoulders that I didn't understand and he kept making the same signal.

I finally whispered my question "big buck?"

"No," said Pat, "big bear."

There was a little strip of alfalfa that ran about 100 yards in length. It was away from the main field and it was loaded with deer tracks. The bear came out and started feeding on the alfalfa. He was there for a while, but then the wind swirled and he stood up on his hind legs. To a guy who'd never seen a bear in the wild before, he looked 20 feet tall! I didn't have a bear tag and I didn't know what the bear would do. I was afraid I might have to shoot him in self defense. He apparently had smelled us, though, and he ran off into the woods.

I figured we wouldn't see any deer now because of the bear. But as it got later, we saw a couple of does and a small buck. There was about five minutes of shooting time remaining when a buck stepped out into the field. I looked at him, and he just didn't look like the big bucks I'm used to seeing in Canada.

It was September and the deer didn't have rut-swollen necks yet. I looked at the height of his tines, though, and they were quite long. He had three tines up on one side, which usually means the deer is a 10-pointer, assuming he's got brow tines. He was definitely a shooter. I had to lean around and go under a tree limb to make the shot. The buck turned out to be a beautiful mainframe 9-pointer with a forked G-2 that grossed 167 points!

# TACTICAL BREAKDOWN

We spotted a little bottleneck of alfalfa off the main field and set up our tree stand there. It looked good because the deer could feed without coming out in the wide open. They'd work toward the big field as it got dark.

I was able to quickly make a decision to take the 10-pointer based on a side look. I never got a front look. I only had one opportunity to take the shot or pass. I saw those three tines up with good tine length and mass and knew the buck was a good one.

## Keys to Success

- Scout to find active food sources.
- Identify a hotspot such as the alfalfa bottleneck where deer feel secure.
- Be prepared to quickly evaluate a buck under less-than-ideal circumstances.

# 10

# First Canadian Buck

**M**y first deer hunting trip to Alberta was with Russell Thornberry. We were there to tape a TV show and asked Russ, who was a hunting outfitter in Alberta before we hired him as editor of *Buckmasters* magazine, to help us out. It was incredibly cold on that trip—it was the third week of November—and we didn't have the tree stands we hunt out of now. Russell had some homemade stands, and he'd put one up so high in a cottonwood that we called it the nose-bleed stand. I must have been 50 feet off the ground up there!

The deer were in full rut, and we were hunting them between their food source and bedding area. The cover was thick, with lots of willow patches. The does were bedding in the willows and the bucks were cutting through there, looking for hot does. This particular morning, we saw a lot of deer. We were

*Credit: Russell Thornberry*

within view of Russell's ranch house, and he was using a spot-
ting scope to see what was happening.

All of a sudden, I caught a glimpse of a pretty good rack
moving in the brush. The rack looked high and wide and the
buck was right on a doe. I didn't have a rangefinder in those
days, but it was a longer shot than I wanted to take. I estimated
the range at 250 to 300 yards. I knew I was looking at a shooter
buck, as the beams on this deer went out past his nose.

I didn't expect to get a shot, but the doe was going to the bedding area so I paid close attention. She turned and came right to me, and the buck came right behind her. I didn't panic, but here comes this buck at 300 yards headed straight toward me. Buck fever was sinking in, and I had to get control of it. I can't tell you how many times I have looked away from a deer to catch my breath while he was working his way to me. I had to relax to make the shot.

The deer came to within 100 yards, but he was walking right toward me and I didn't like that angle. Russell was watching from the front porch, trying to figure out why I hadn't shot. When the buck walked by me, I finally got a good angle. I put the crosshairs right on him and shot. He jumped, ran 30 yards, stopped broadside, and I shot him again. This time he ran about 40 yards and dropped. Both shots were right behind the shoulder. He should have dropped after the first shot, but he was too

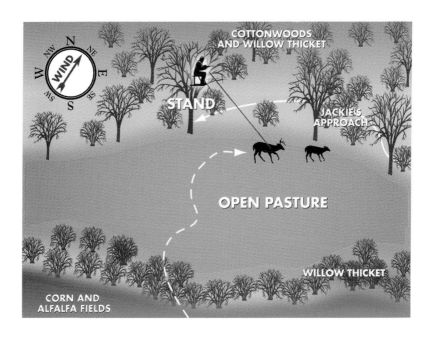

pumped up by the rut. Their will to live is phenomenal! He was a very nice buck—close to 160 inches—and my first Canadian deer for television. His beams came around and almost touched at the tips. It's a unique rack. That's one of the interesting things about whitetails. No two bucks are exactly alike.

# TACTICAL BREAKDOWN

When the rut is going full bore, you can't go wrong hunting near a concentration of does. If you hunt where the does are, there's a good chance you'll see good buck activity. That's what happened on this deer. He found his doe, and she was going back to her bedding area.

It's also important when the deer is not disturbed and is moving toward you to be patient and wait for your shot. I was tempted several times to try a long shot, but I held out and wound up with a close shot.

## Keys to Success

- During the rut, hunt where the does are. The bucks will be near the does during breeding season.
- Fight buck fever by looking away from the deer and taking deep breaths.
- Be patient; wait until you have a high percentage shot.

# 11

# A Buck That Was Meant to Be

We went up to hunt familiar territory in Alberta during the fall of 2000, and we timed things just right. The deer were in the rut, and bucks were chasing does all day long. They weren't out in the fields all day, but they were moving back in the cottonwoods. Because the deer were so active, we stayed in our tree stands all day.

We'd seen some pretty good deer the first two days of our three-day hunt. We had one tree stand in a willow thicket that was tight to the bedding area that we usually hunt. There was a big slough lined with cottonwood trees that went through the area. The bucks were scraping along that tree line constantly.

*Credit: Gene Bidlespacher*

We'd seen a pretty nice 8-pointer, and I told my producer, Gene Bidlespacher, that if we got another chance at that 8-pointer, we'd take him. On the last afternoon of our hunt, the deer were still active. I was talking to Gene, and he reminded me about my plan to shoot the 8-pointer. I reminded Gene that if that deer came, I would take him.

"Well, look right below you," said Gene. The 8-pointer had snuck up behind us, and was now looking right up in the tree at us! We got it all on video. Then Gene whispered, "what are you going to do?" I told him I'd changed my mind—I'd decided not to shoot that buck. "Okay," said Gene, "but you're going to run out of time."

It's amazing how often you get a good buck in the last 10 minutes of a hunt, and this hunt was coming down to our last 10 minutes. It's important to know the legal shooting times, and we always pay close attention to that detail. It's also important to maintain your concentration until the hunt is over.

If we didn't get a deer on this particular afternoon, we would have to fly home and come back the next week. I was thinking about that when I caught a glimpse of a doe cutting through the thicket above us, and then I saw a buck behind the doe. It was obviously a shooter.

The deer were paralleling the thicket, walking along the edge. The cover was thick and I had to wait for a hole to shoot through. The buck kept walking, never slowing, never stopping. With our camera setup, Gene only had a certain amount of room where his camera would swivel, and I could see that he was running out of room. The deer finally got out in front of me and I found one hole in the cover. I grunted when he got there and he stopped, looking our way. I made the shot and the deer, a

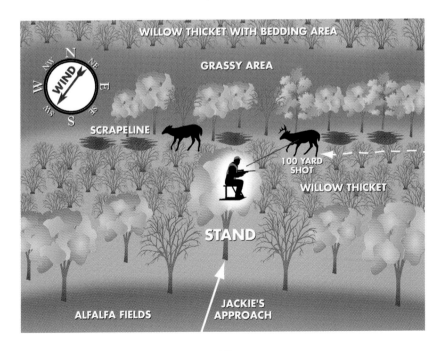

150-inch 10-pointer, took off immediately. His tail was tucked when he ran, though, so I knew he was hit hard.

Gene and I just sat there and looked at each other. There were five minutes of shooting light left on the last afternoon and we'd been passing deer after deer for three days. It was one of those bucks that was meant to be. We had taken a deer from the same setup the previous year, and that deer was also taken in the last five minutes of the hunt.

# TACTICAL BREAKDOWN

We were set up in a thick spot where there was a lot of rutting activity—lots of scrapes, and bucks actively chasing does during daylight hours. We also had the wind right for our setup. When the rut is that strong, you should stay in your stand from daylight until dark.

In this case, it was nearly dark when I shot the deer, but he could have come by any time. I had to be patient and wait for an opening where the buck would stop for a shot. If you grunt at a deer and you don't have an opening for a shot, you put him on alert for no reason.

## Keys to Success

- Hunt during the rut whenever you can.
- Set up in an area of intense rutting activity.
- Hunt all day during the rut, no matter what the weather is like.
- Be selective about the buck you harvest.
- Wait for a good shot.
- Know the legal shooting times.
- Maintain your concentration.

# 12

# Bottleneck Buck

There are some food sources that attract whitetails like a candy store attracts kids. The sugar beet is one of those foods. We bowhunted in Montana one October when the sugar beets were being harvested. We'd hunted that property for several years, and we had a pretty good idea which routes the deer took to and from the fields.

The farmers in that area rotate their crops. One year they plant a field in beets, the next year corn, the next alfalfa. This particular year, the beets were in a field that worked well for us because the deer were funneled into a bottleneck between the bedding area and the field. The weather was practically balmy when we started hunting, but a big cold front blew in once we were there. In one afternoon, it went from 50°F with a 15-mph

*Credit: Gene Bidlespacher*

wind to 5°F with a 30-mph wind. I didn't expect that kind of weather in October, and didn't bring enough warm clothes.

We had two afternoon tree stands called Alan 1 and Alan 2. They were pretty close to the bedding area. The deer came through a big willow thicket past both of those stands. Deer that came from the top of the thicket passed by one stand and those that came from the bottom of the thicket passed by the other.

It seemed like whichever stand we chose, the deer came by the other one. For a while, I considered putting a dummy in the stand I wasn't hunting. I always let Gene Bidlespacher make the call on which stand to hunt, and that way I can blame him if things go wrong.

It was early in the year, and the bucks were still running together. Late in the afternoon, we saw movement in the thicket and a big 9-pointer walked out, moving at an angle that would take him past Alan 2. Of course, we were hunting in Alan 1. Pretty soon, here came a big 10-pointer and another big 9. There were three shooter bucks together and they were all going to pass within range of the empty stand.

Gene and I just shook our heads. Just when it seemed as if all was lost, a doe walked out of the thicket on our end, and came right toward our stand. One of those bucks looked up, saw the doe, and started walking toward her. It was way too early for the rut, but he was definitely coming to investigate the doe. The other two bucks wandered off toward the beet field.

The doe came right past us, and the buck was heading the same way. We were set up parallel to a deer trail about 20 yards away, and the buck got on that trail and turned broadside. Gene

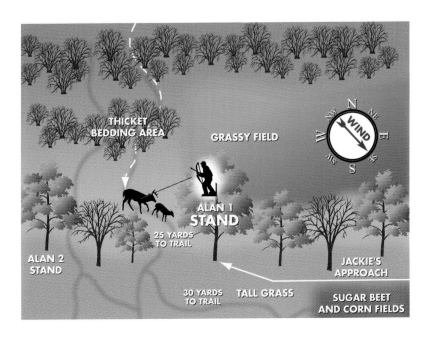

whispered that he had the deer on camera and I drew my bow and grunted, but the buck never stopped. He probably didn't hear me in the 30-mph wind. As the deer walked along the trail, he got to a spot where my body blocked the camera from following the buck. Gene told me not to shoot, but I didn't hear him in the wind. I grunted again, this time real loud, and the buck stopped—and when he stopped, I let him have it. He's a 137-inch 9-pointer with beams that turn up, a beautiful deer. The other two bucks that he was traveling with were every bit as big, maybe bigger.

# TACTICAL BREAKDOWN

We knew we had a real deer magnet with all those sugar beets, we'd hunted and scouted the same fields for several years; and we knew how the deer moved to them. The deer activity was good, but a major cold front had the deer feeding even more actively. It snowed seven inches the night after I shot that buck.

Our blinds were well located within 20 yards of the major trails that led from bedding areas to feeding areas.

## Keys to Success

- Work with a landowner to know when he plans to harvest favored deer foods such as sugar beets.
- Set up blinds within shooting range of major trails.
- Play the weather. Deer often feed actively when cold weather is approaching.
- Stay alert to potential shots. Bucks in October shouldn't be interested in does, but this one was.
- Hunt near bedding areas in the afternoon.

# 13

# Mountain Laurel Monster

W e've hunted several times in Pennsylvania with an operation called Hill Country Whitetails. Their property is a neat place to bowhunt. The cover is very thick, with dense stands of mountain laurel higher than a man's head and wicked vines that we call "whoa, here" vines because when you get stuck on one, you're gonna whoa, here! You have to get 25 feet up in a tree to understand why the deer like to move through that mountain laurel. They're well protected in the thick cover.

This hunting operation plants grain sorghum and clover fields for the deer. There's also a lot of native browse plus, in the fall, acorns. We hunted there in October one year and really did our

Credit: George Warner

homework. We found a nice woodlot next to a sorghum field. The woodlot was about 100 yards wide by 500 yards long and we set up a stand where a game trail forked off an old road. The deer had been scraping all along the road, and it looked like a great spot.

We first hunted that stand in the morning and saw a number of bucks moving through the area and working scrapes. There was a lot of buck activity. The only bad thing about the stand is that our tree was covered with vines that I was pretty sure were poison sumac. I'm allergic to poison ivy, poison oak, and poison sumac and, although it was warm on this hunt, I wore gloves to protect myself as I was climbing the ladder to the stand. I was so thoroughly covered that I was certain I wouldn't have a problem. Wrong! Not only did I get poison sumac, I was consumed with it for almost four months. I even had it in my eyes.

Luckily, the itching didn't start until after I got my deer. We were hunting the stand in the afternoon and had seen several does when a nice buck stepped out in the old road and started our way. He went right to a scrape and started working it. It was great, because the buck did everything you hear about and read about and we were getting it all on video. He was putting on a show on what a deer is supposed to do at a scrape. He even stood up on his hind legs and rubbed his head and face in the branches above the scrape.

Once the buck finished scraping, he started walking up the road right to us. It was a good situation because we had the wind in our face. If he stayed in the road, I would have a good shot. Even if the deer turned off on the game trail, I'd still get a good shot at him. The buck really took his time and finally cut off on the trail. He was committed, just moving slowly along the trail.

When he got to about 20 yards, I waited until he walked behind some brush and drew my bow. I grunted when he walked

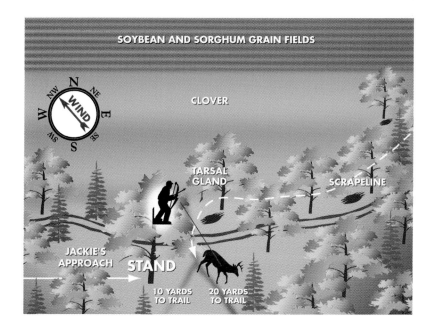

out from behind the brush, and he stopped broadside. It was a classic setup that worked just the way it was supposed to work, and I was fortunate to make a good shot on that buck. He didn't go far. He was a respectable 8-pointer that scored about 130. I've shot much bigger bucks, but I'll never forget that Pennsylvania deer, because of the great video, because of the poison sumac, and because of the ideal setup. We were successful three years in a row in that same stand.

# TACTICAL BREAKDOWN

We did our homework on this hunt, studying an aerial photo to locate a woodlot next to a feeding field. Scouting revealed active buck scrapes in an old road inside the woodlot. We found an ideal tree for a stand at the intersection of the road and a game trail.

With the wind in our favor, it was a perfect setup. All I had to remember when it came time for the shot was to wait until the deer couldn't see me move before drawing my bow. I used a grunt to stop the buck for the shot.

## Keys to Success

- Do your homework before the hunt. An aerial photo is always a useful tool because it allows you to identify feeding areas, bedding areas, and bottlenecks.
- Put a stand at the intersection of two trails. This increases your odds of getting a close shot.
- Don't draw your bow or move if the deer can see you. Wait until the deer turns his head or moves behind a tree or a bush.

# Bucks on Camera

## *Footage from Buckmasters Hunts*

This buck had just come from a watering hole. Water holes can pay off
when the weather is hot. (Chapter 21—"Best Texas Buck Ever.")

This is the famous drop-tine buck. He stopped when I grunted at him. This is seconds before the shot. (Chapter 1—"The Drop Tine Buck.")

This 171-inch Iowa monster is fleeing after being shot with my Knight muzzleloader. (Chapter 2—"Consolation Prize.")

This big 10-point South Texas buck is chasing does. Minutes later, he came back out and I had the shot. (Chapter 22—"Drought Buck.")

This big 9-point Idaho buck has just stood up from bedding behind the big rock. The shot followed quickly.

This 10-point Mexico whitetail is seconds from being shot. I aimed right in front of his shoulder and squeezed the shot off. (Chapter 23—"Running 10-Pointer.")

An 8-point Alabama buck is doing a little lip curling before being taken with a shotgun slug.

This is the biggest buck that I've ever taken on video in Alabama. The 9-point buck was walking when I grunted to make him stop. The shot followed immediately. (Chapter 15—"Best Alabama Buck on Video.")

My first big buck in Illinois with guide Ron Doering. It was taken with a shot-gun and had 167 inches of antler. (Chapter 3—"The Off-Camera Buck.")

This 10-point Montana buck is seconds from being hit with my arrow as he walks by our treestand. (Chapter 4—"Bruiser Buck With a Bow.")

My first Saskatchewan buck taken on video with a rifle. The buck is look-ing at the does running off. The shot followed. (Chapter 34—"First Saskatchewan Rifle Buck on TV.")

This wide-racked 8-pointer has just cleared a big tree to my left, in the foreground, and has given me a perfect broadside shot.

This Montana 9-point buck stopped in his tracks when I grunted at him. The arrow was released within seconds. (Chapter 35—"Late-Morning Buck.")

A 10-point Texas buck crosses a clover field, where he had been feeding. He has 160 inches of antler, and was taken with a rifle seconds after this shot was taken.

This Canadian buck has just stopped when I grunted. The buck was taken as he was moving from one woodlot to another, and had 170 inches of antler. (Chapter 7—"The Woodlot Buck.")

This Canadian giant is the biggest 8-point buck I've ever taken. He had 160 inches of antler. (Chapter 8—"Woodline 8-Pointer.")

As the buck looked away, I drew my bow. A 10-pointer, this Montana monster was a great bow buck. (Chapter 25—"Late Bow Buck.")

As this Pennsylvania buck cleared the tree, he offered me my shot. (Chapter 26—"Borderline Buck.")

This Pennsylvania 9-pointer is not giving me a shot right here. After standing still for almost thirty minutes, watching some nearby does, he finally stepped into the open, and I made the shot. He weighed 260 pounds!

I had to pick a hole to shoot at this Canadian 10-pointer. (Chapter 11—"A Buck That Was Meant to Be.")

This buck was right under our stand. I grunted to make him stop before I released my arrow. He was a 9-pointer with 135 inches of antler. (Chapter 12—"Bottleneck Buck.")

My first record buck in Saskatchewan with a bow. He was coming in to freshen up his scrapes. (Chapter 33—"Record Buck at -30°F.")

This heavy-beamed Alabama buck was at 20 yards when cutting through a bottleneck strip of hardwoods. He was taken with a shotgun slug. (Chapter 16—"Scrapeline Buck With a Shotgun.")

This wide 8-pointer has just turned broadside and given me a perfect 70-yard shot.

This big 8-pointer was going from scrape to scrape. One more step, then the arrow found its target. (Chapter 13—"Mountain Laurel Monster.")

Imperial Clover fields are the favorite afternoon food source for these deer. This 10-point buck was taken with a shotgun at 80 yards. (Chapter 14—"Phone Pole Buck.")

This monster 8-pointer stepped out of a bottleneck just at dusk, giving me a perfect broadside shot. (Chapter 19—"The Flexibility Factor.")

# 14

# Phone Pole Buck

On our hunting club land in Alabama, we plant 15 to 20 small fields in Imperial Whitetail Clover. Deer really like to feed on clover. We keep the fields small—one or two acres—and that makes them easier to hunt. Big fields, like the ones farmers or ranchers plant for crops or livestock feed, are harder to hunt because the deer have too many places they can enter. You can usually see the deer in large fields, but they're generally too far for a shot. Keeping the fields small also makes the deer feel more secure because they're not far from cover, even in the middle of the field.

We have one field we call Rabbit Alley. It's surrounded by a clear-cut that was planted in thick pine trees. There used to be a big dead tree in the middle of the Rabbit Alley, but it was

*Credit: Gene Bidlespacher*

knocked down by a tornado, so we lost that as a stand site. There's a good bottleneck coming off the pine plantation to the clover field, but there aren't any trees suitable for a stand in there. One solution was to set up a ground blind on the field. Anytime we hunt there, we see a lot of deer coming from the bottleneck. There are four major trails in that area, and we needed to set up a bow stand right there.

I have a friend from high school who works for the telephone company. I managed to get a 40-foot telephone pole, and my friend brought in a big auger and we set up that pole right in the bottleneck, 10 feet deep. We positioned the pole between two cedar trees, and then put our tree stands on the pole. You can hunt those stands with a rifle, shotgun, or bow. I was using a shotgun on this particular hunt.

It was an afternoon hunt on a north-northwest wind. I looked at my aerial photo, as I always do, and decided that the wind direction was right for hunting out of the utility pole. It got to be late afternoon, and we were watching does and young bucks in the field when all the deer looked up and started looking back at the thicket.

Reading whitetail body language, I felt pretty sure a bigger buck was heading toward the field. If a young buck is looking at an approaching doe, he'll look long enough to identify the deer as a doe, then he'll return to feeding. If there's a bigger buck coming, a young buck will watch him with more concern because he's afraid. I could see legs walking through the thicket and I got a glimpse of antler tips. Then the buck stepped into the edge of the field, and I knew he was a shooter right away.

I'd already used my rangefinder to figure the distances where I expected to see a buck, and it was 100 yards to that deer. My shotgun is accurate at that range, but I decided to see what would happen. The deer fed out into the field and then came

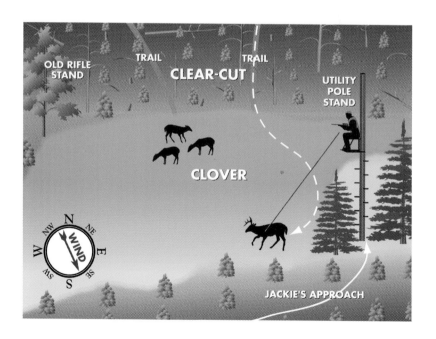

toward us. When he got to about 60 yards, he was plenty close. All I had to do was wait until he turned broadside and concentrate on making a good shot. That buck had great mass and nearly 140 inches of antler. That's big for an Alabama whitetail.

# TACTICAL BREAKDOWN

Sometimes you have to be creative when you're setting up a deer stand. I positioned a utility pole at exactly the location I wanted, and put tree stands on it. It worked out great. Our clover patches are excellent for afternoon hunts.

I never go deer hunting without checking wind direction, which is critical for determining which stand to hunt and how you approach the stand. Being able to read whitetail body language tipped me that a shooter buck was coming before I could see him. Finally, I knew my effective shotgun range and waited for a good shot.

## Keys to Success

- Be creative when setting up deer stands.
- Take advantage of food plots that attract deer.
- Know your effective range.
- Choose stands based on wind direction.
- When the target deer is undisturbed, wait for a high percentage shot.

# 15

# Best Alabama Buck on Video

By Alabama standards, we had a very cold fall and winter in 2000. The cold weather really affected our clover fields. In fact, the clover didn't pay off for most of the season. By the last week of January, 2001, we got a little warm-up and a nice rain. In whitetail hunting, you need to pay attention to weather conditions and how the deer adapt to the changes.

Our dormant clover started to grow in the warmer weather, and the deer really piled onto the fields. We went to an afternoon stand on a small place I'd bought. We'd never taken a deer off the property, but we'd planted soybeans and clover for groceries and let the deer grow. Our stand was bordering a clover

*Credit: Gene Bidlespacher*

field, in a water oak tree that had a lot of Spanish moss hanging in it. The Spanish moss really helped break up our outline in the tree. You should always try to utilize natural cover such as this, no matter where you hunt.

We were in a little funnel, and we could get to the stand without detection if we were careful. There were bedding areas on either side of us; they weren't far away, and we made a concerted effort to be extra quiet approaching and climbing into the stand. That afternoon, I spotted a nice buck that wasn't quite big enough to shoot. We also had several does and other small bucks in the field.

As it started getting dark, I saw the does in the field throw up their heads and look back at the thicket. I heard a deer grunt; so did Gene Bidlespacher, my producer and cameraman. It was too dark to shoot, but we couldn't get out of the stand because we didn't want to spook that deer. The deer came out onto the field and I looked at him through my binoculars. Even though it was dark, I could see a great frame with good mass, and I could make out a crab claw point at the end of his beam. Gene couldn't see the deer, and I told him I thought it was a 140-inch buck.

The buck came within 40 yards of the stand, chased the does, and then went to a scrape. We stayed in the stand for an hour after dark to avoid spooking him. Then we got down quietly and circled away so we could get back to the four-wheelers without disturbing him.

We came back two afternoons later. Unfortunately, we had an east wind, which didn't work at all for the setup where we'd seen the big buck. We went to another nearby clover field instead. There, the two of us watched the usual parade of does and small bucks until 30 minutes before dark, when a good buck stepped into the field about as far from our stand as he could get. I knew

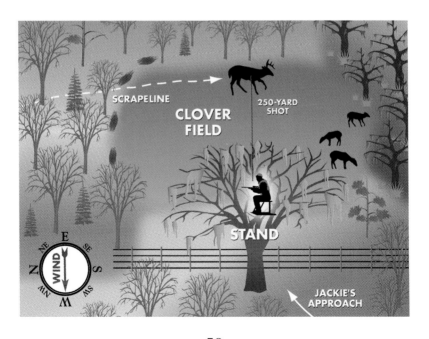

from using my rangefinder previously that it was 250 yards to the edge of the cover; the buck was about 240 yards away.

That's a long shot, and I made sure that I had a good rest for my rifle and a solid rest for my elbow. The buck got broadside to us and started walking, so I grunted to stop him. He ran when I shot, but I could see his tail twitch and I felt pretty confident that I'd made a good shot. He went about 40 yards into the cover and went down. It was the same buck we'd seen the night before! I knew, because he had that distinctive crab claw point. It just goes to show that the bucks can get big anywhere if they have enough to eat and time to grow. That's the best Alabama buck we'd shot on video, and I was particularly proud because he was a product of my own, personal management program.

# TACTICAL BREAKDOWN

I paid attention to changing weather conditions that created a growth spurt in a dormant food source. We approached our stand cautiously to avoid alerting nearby deer, and we stayed in our stand an hour after dark to avoid spooking the target buck we'd seen.

Changing wind conditions made it impractical to hunt the same stand on the next hunt, so we set up on a nearby clover field where the wind was in our favor. When I made the long shot, I concentrated on getting a solid rest for both my rifle and my elbow.

## Keys to Success

- Pay attention to changing weather that affects food sources.
- Approach and leave stands cautiously to avoid spooking deer.
- Abandon a favored stand if the wind is not right.
- Get the best possible rifle rest to make an accurate shot.

# 16

# Scrapeline Buck With a Shotgun

Whitetails love edges. They like places where two or more types of habitats meet. The plant diversity is usually good in those situations, so they have a variety of browse to choose from. Since edges usually involve heavy cover, deer have convenient escape routes. Edges can be where a woodlot meets a planted field, or they can be much more subtle.

For instance, on our hunting lease in Alabama, we've got a productive stand where a strip of hardwoods meets a clear-cut that's been replanted in pines. The clear-cut surrounds the hardwoods on three sides, forming a bottleneck. We set up our stand in a tight situation so it can serve for muzzleloader,

*Credit: Gene Bidlespacher*

shotgun, or archery hunting. The major trails come out of the pines to our right, cutting across the hardwoods and going back into the pines.

From scouting, we know that the bucks make scrapes down a row of pines about two or three rows back into the plantation. They move back and forth in that thick pine plantation and are never exposed. If I could only hunt one type of habitat in Alabama, I would choose two- to five-year-old clear-cuts. It's perfect habitat because it has everything the deer need and offers them good protection. They never have to leave the clear-cuts. They've got food and bedding cover both in the same spot.

This particular stand was a good setup for any type of north wind, but it was best when the wind was from the northwest. On this particular hunt, we got into the stand on a quiet morning, about 30 minutes before daylight. The rut was on. As soon as it was daylight, we started seeing does moving through. With that many does and a scrapeline close by, we knew there was a good chance of seeing a mature buck.

Gene Bidlespacher saw a buck come out of the thicket on the right side of the blind onto the road. I'm left-handed and the deer was behind me, about 50 yards away. I didn't know if he was going to head up the road or cut across, so I was trying to look around without moving to see which way he was going. The buck finally committed and started right for us. He was going to cut across, get to the other trail, and go up that scrapeline.

He was a big-bodied buck, over 200 pounds, and he had a nice rack. I eased around as much as I could, got my shotgun rested on my knee, and got set up to shoot the deer when he crossed an opening. He was so close—probably 20 steps—that I didn't even grunt at him. When he got to the opening, I took the

shot. I could see where the shotgun slug hit him, and he didn't go far.

# TACTICAL BREAKDOWN

Our scouting revealed an active scrapeline near the stand and the rut was going full bore. There are a lot of does in that area. During the rut, hunt near concentrations of does, because bucks will always be close by.

Our setup was ideal for shotgun hunting because visibility was limited and I couldn't take a long shot, anyway. I picked an opening that I thought the buck would walk through and waited for him to get to that open spot before taking the shot.

## Keys to Success

- Scout to find active deer sign.
- Scrapes are the best sign to indicate the immediate presence of bucks.
- Hunt near does during the rut.
- Set up stands in tight cover to accommodate short-range shots from shotguns, muzzleloaders, and bows.

# 17

# Muzzleloader Buck

**M**ature bucks can be extremely sensitive to any change in their habitat, so I prefer not to make changes during the hunting season. Occasionally, though, you can get away with a slight alteration. On the hunting club I belong to in Alabama, we set up a stand specifically to use for close-range hunting with a muzzleloader, bow, or shotgun.

We call this stand the "Muzzleloader Woods Stand," and it's set up in a little strip of hardwoods flanked on three sides by a clear-cut replanted in pine. It was given that name because the first two bucks we shot there were taken with a muzzleloader. Those deer stayed back in the pines most of the time. When they wanted to move, they cut across the stand of hardwoods and re-entered the pines on the other side.

*Credit: Gene Bidlespacher*

We had seen a good buck one morning when it was extremely still. I can't hear very well, but my producer Gene Bidlespacher sure can. Gene heard the deer grunting before we got a glimpse of him walking through the pines, but he was too far back in the trees for a shot. From what we could tell, he was working a scrapeline about two or three rows back in the pine plantation.

After the hunt that morning, I took a saw into the pines and limbed out a few trees. I was very selective about what I cut. I just wanted to open up a few holes where we could see a little better. Then we bailed out and stayed away from the stand for three days. Sometimes when you change the habitat, you can stay away for a couple of days and let the deer get used to the change.

66

Even when you're playing the wind direction just right, an old buck that's already seen something he doesn't like might go the other way if he hears a four-wheeler before daylight or hears the slightest noise made by a hunter climbing into a tree stand.

We gave the Muzzleloader Tree Stand some time to cool down, then went back in for a morning hunt. Sure enough, we saw the buck again, this time moving inside the protective pines from the opposite direction he'd been going the first time we saw him. I got lined up on one of the shooting lanes I'd made and grunted when the buck got there. When I shot, all I could see was smoke from the muzzleloader. Compared to a centerfire rifle, a muzzleloader has a slight delay between pulling the trigger and ignition of the powder. You have to hang in there for what I call the follow-through to make certain your shot is accurate.

When I got down from the stand, I walked to where the deer was and didn't see any blood. Then I started moving in the

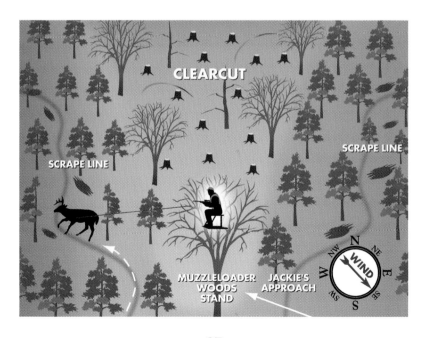

direction I thought the deer went, and I could smell the buck almost immediately. Rutting bucks have a very strong odor, and I was downwind of him. Within 10 steps, I saw him lying there. He was a nice 9-point with a real heavy rack.

# TACTICAL BREAKDOWN

We had a good setup that we had thoroughly scouted. I was hunting with a muzzleloader, and selected a stand where I knew the shot would be close. In order to see a buck in the thick vegetation, I selectively trimmed a few limbs to create shooting lanes; then we stayed away from the spot and gave the deer time to get used to the changes.

When you shoot a muzzleloader, you have to concentrate to stay on target until the powder ignites. I aim behind the shoulder at the lower one-third of the deer's body because I'm more likely to shoot high with a muzzleloader. When conditions are right, you can smell a buck from downwind.

## Keys to Success

- Scout your hunting area to learn how deer move. This is particularly important in dense cover where you don't have long to make the shot.
- If you must trim shooting lanes during hunting season, make as few changes as possible.
- Give the deer time to adapt to habitat changes.
- Follow through with a muzzleloader—concentrate to stay on target.
- Despite our relatively poor sense of smell, it's sometimes possible for a hunter to smell a buck.

# 18

# My Son's First Major Buck

I started taking my son, Jackie, to tree stands with me when he was 4 or 5 years old. I just wanted him to sit in the stand and see what deer hunting was all about. I felt that I was exposing him to the outdoors without pressuring him to become a hunter. Those days were priceless. Jackie would usually fall asleep in the stand and I'd wake him up, foggy-eyed, when a deer came by. Jackie would get excited when he'd see a deer, and the whole experience was very special for mc.

When Jackie got a little older, he shot BB guns and then a scoped .22 rifle. An accurate .22 is a great teaching tool for a youngster. There's no recoil, not much noise, and the ammuni-

Credit: Elliott Allen

tion is inexpensive. We were in a blind together at the end of the hunting season when Jackie was 8. A nice, young 10-pointer came into the field and Jackie really got excited. He tried to talk me into shooting the deer, but we needed to let that one grow up a little more. I could see that he was excited, though, and I asked him if he was ready to shoot a buck. He said yes and we went to work to get ready for the next season.

Jackie was 9 that fall, and I got him a Remington Model 7 in .243 caliber. That's a great youth gun because it's small enough for a kid to handle and has light recoil, but is an efficient caliber for deer hunting. He got a spike buck that year out of the field we call Rabbit Alley, and I'll never forget that buck.

Jackie got a small buck the next year and again the year after that. Every time we hunted, we talked about the wind situation, studied the aerial photos, and made our stand selections. We were having fun, but it was a learning experience, as well.

The season Jackie was 12, we went out together on Thanksgiving afternoon. The holidays are times for being with family, and we do most of our hunting together during the Thanksgiving and Christmas holidays when Jackie is out of school. For me, Thanksgiving has always been a lucky time, and Jackie apparently inherited my lucky gene. It was a special afternoon for both of us. We climbed up in a box blind that was really too small for two people. I had a video camera to film the hunt. A small buck came out on the field. When I was 12, I'd shoot anything with antlers, but Jackie decided to pass that buck and wait for a bigger one.

It was getting dark when I saw a buck step out into the edge of the field. It was a good buck. Jackie got his rifle up and found the deer in the scope. I was so excited I couldn't handle

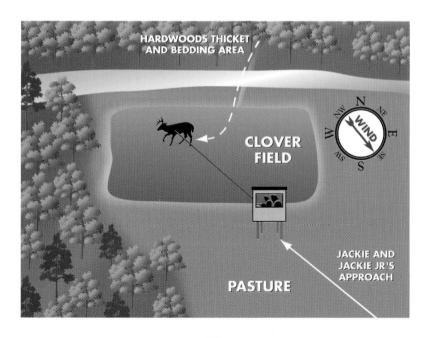

the camera—I had to put it down! When Jackie shot, the buck just hit the ground.

We got out of the stand and walked over to the deer. The closer we got, the bigger it looked. That buck was a 9-pointer with a 22-inch spread and six-inch bases. It was the biggest buck that had been taken off that property in 25 years. That's an experience that's etched in my memory forever. Never pass up a chance to spend time in the outdoors with your kids.

# TACTICAL BREAKDOWN

When you introduce a youth to hunting, let the youth decide when he or she is ready. Don't force them to hunt or you'll turn them off. Teach your kids to shoot an air rifle and a .22 rifle first. Don't let them shoot a big-bore deer rifle until they're ready. The noise and recoil will discourage them from shooting, and encourage flinching.

Most kids can't sit still for long periods of time. They'll have more fun hunting quail, doves, ducks, squirrels, or rabbits. There's a lot more action, and action holds their attention. Many youths who start on small game will come around to deer hunting later.

## Keys to Success

- Don't push kids into hunting.
- Once kids are comfortable with air rifles and .22 rifles, give them a lighter caliber deer rifle for their first actual hunt. Such rifles are easy to handle and have mild recoil.

# 19

# The Flexibility Factor

**M**ost whitetail hunters understand they're better off hunting from some form of elevated stand. Being above the deer gets your scent off the ground, where the air currents will hopefully keep your scent from spooking the deer. Ideally, you improve your field of view by being above the deer, though that doesn't always work. Finally, deer are less likely to see you when you're higher up than they are.

I mostly hunt from tree stands, and I always have a cameraman along. Because of that, we're putting out twice as much scent and we've got twice as much movement as a lone hunter. And don't think that deer won't see you because you're 25 or 30 feet above them. I don't care how high up you are, if you're sit-

Credit: Gene Bidlespacher

ting in the open and the deer look up, they've got you pegged. And they *will* look up.

On our Alabama hunting club land, we have a nice clover field with a stand location on a fencerow that works well for rifle hunting. The deer come into that field from the other end, and I really wanted to put a stand in that area for hunting with a bow, shotgun, or muzzleloader. There were no suitable trees, so I put up another one of my utility poles and put the stand on that.

We situated the pole in a hedgerow about 100 yards from a very active creek crossing. There was a tall tree behind us with Spanish moss in the limbs to give us some cover. The moss would break our silhouette. There was another clover field about 350 yards away, and it seemed like whichever field we hunted a good buck always showed up in the other field. We hunted one afternoon and saw a nice rack buck in the far field. The next day we got the wind direction we needed, and we shifted our attention to that field, hunting from the telephone pole stand.

The deer started to move late in the afternoon. We had four or five does come into the field and start feeding. It was getting late when I saw a good buck come out across the creek and go to a scrape. He worked it over, rubbing his head in the limbs and doing the whole ritual. He was only 80 yards away, but I didn't have a shot. I was getting a little concerned because the does in the field were feeding around and were almost downwind of us. The air was cooling, and I knew the late-afternoon thermals would push our scent downward.

Luckily, the buck saw those does, crossed the creek, and came out into the field to check them out. He got about 60 to 65 yards from the blind and I let him have it with my shotgun. Shotgun slugs really pound a deer. This old buck was a good, mature buck and probably weighed 220 pounds. He ran back the way he'd come, but piled up not far past the creek.

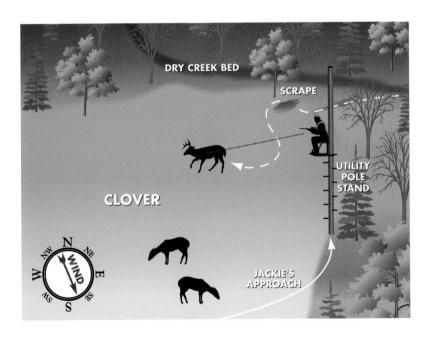

# TACTICAL BREAKDOWN

We like to stay as flexible as possible and have a number of stand locations that work well in changing wind conditions. We first spotted this buck from a stand on another field 350 yards away, then moved into position to hunt him when the wind was favorable.

Again, we put a telephone pole in place for a suitable tree stand location. We made our stand less noticeable by putting it in front of a tree that had Spanish moss hanging from its limbs. The tree background and the Spanish moss moving in the breeze helped conceal two men on a telephone pole.

## Keys to Success

- Stay flexible, with as many stand locations as possible.
- When practical, be on the lookout for deer in the distance and relocate to intercept them.
- Always check wind direction and select a stand that favors the wind.
- Use natural cover to break up your outline, even when you are hunting high above the ground.

# 20

# Clear-Cut 8-Pointer

One season, in early January, I found a regrowth clear-cut thicket on our Alabama hunting lease that was loaded with deer sign. There were lots of tracks, a good scrapeline, and innumerable rubs. It looked like a good place to take a buck, so we set up two stands, one to use on a north wind, one on a south wind.

The clear-cut was grown up in green briars and honeysuckle, so the deer had browse. It was surrounded by pine and hardwood thickets, so they had cover too. In fact, the regrowth was so thick that you couldn't see the deer unless you got up high. The stand we used on a south wind was way up in a big oak tree.

When we got in the woods that morning, I checked the wind direction and saw that it was out of the south. On that particular setup, we were hunting very close to a bedding area and

*Credit: Pat Gregory*

the approach to the stand was critical. We came in through a swamp and quietly got in the stand about 30 minutes before daylight. Making a silent approach to the stand is critical. Otherwise, you spook deer that are in the area. If I have to walk to my stand through thick woods, I sometimes wait until first light so I can see where I'm going and walk quieter. I'd rather miss prime hunting time than make too much noise.

We saw a lot of deer movement early but it was all does and small bucks. About 9:00 a.m., I heard a racket that I'd never heard before. Pat Gregory, my cameraman that day, and I both thought we were hearing a four-wheeler running. We finally realized it was a buck grunting as he chased a doe, but the sound was unlike anything I've ever heard. We could hear limbs breaking and I could visualize the chase.

Listening carefully is a valuable tool for deer hunters and, though I didn't see the deer, I was able to follow the chase by the sounds. I finally heard a soft grunt that sounded more like the buck grunts I was accustomed to, and I knew something was about to happen. The thing about soft grunts is that you don't know if they're being made by a spike or a big buck. Even though I didn't know what kind of buck I was about to see, the anticipation really got me going.

I finally spotted the chase in the edge of the pines and instantly identified the deer as a shooter buck. He stayed behind the pines and never gave me a shot. Then the chase moved into the clear-cut. At one point the deer were 50 yards away, but I

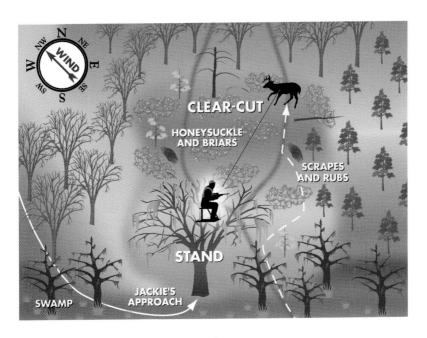

didn't have a shot. I finally picked out a clearing in the direction the chase was headed and got my scope onto the spot. When the buck came roaring into the clearing, I grunted and he stopped in his tracks. I made a good shot and knocked him down. That buck was one of the best 8-pointers we took in the early days of the television show.

# TACTICAL BREAKDOWN

A careful approach to the stand was critical on this hunt because our setup was so close to the bedding area. We had done our scouting, however, and knew how to approach the stand on a south wind without spooking the deer. Not only would the stand have been different on a north wind, the approach would have been different.

That location was excellent for deer because of the edge effect. We had edge where the clear-cut met the pines and edge where the clear-cut met the hardwoods. There was plenty of food and plenty of cover. Listening and knowing what we were hearing was important. Most of the time, we could not see the buck, but we monitored his movements by sounds.

## Keys to Success

- Approach your stand carefully to avoid spooking nearby deer.
- Study wind direction to select which stand to hunt and also how to approach the stand.
- Scout your stand site and look for edge that attracts whitetails.
- Listen carefully for sounds of deer activity.

# 21

# Best Texas Buck Ever

White-tailed deer respond extremely well to a good management program and Texas is the perfect example. There are ranches all over the state where wildlife managers are planting food plots to give the deer nutritious food sources. They're also allowing bucks to grow to maturity before hunting them. Along the way, they judiciously harvest management bucks that have undesirable antler characteristics. The result is big bucks in places you might not expect them.

My friend Don Montgomery has done a great job of deer management in Jack County, north of Dallas. We've hunted with Don several times and we've always seen good deer. Don's mama is quite a deer hunter in her own right. In fact, she once took a 195-inch buck. She's serious. When she sees a buck she

Credit: Gene Bidlespacher

wants, she'll hunt that deer all season, and pass up a lot of other good bucks in the process.

We went down to Montgomery Properties one year and caught weather that was unusually hot. Warm weather is not uncommon when you're hunting Texas or Mexico, but it must have been 90°F that trip. On our first afternoon, Don put us in a box blind overlooking a clover field.

I noticed a water hole in the corner of the field, but I didn't pay much attention to it at first. As the afternoon cooled off, deer started coming out into the field. We saw some decent bucks, but I seldom shoot a buck the first day of the hunt, particularly on a ranch like Don's where I know there are a lot of big bucks.

As we sat there watching deer in the field, a good buck came out of a tree line, walked over, and started working a scrape. Then the deer started walking down the fenceline and came through a gap into the field. He was walking fast and was not heading toward the food source. At first, I couldn't figure out what he was doing. Then I realized he was headed to the water. The warmer the weather, the more attention you should pay to water sources. One of the features I always look for on an aerial photo is water sources. The fewer water sources that your hunting property has, the easier it is to pinpoint where deer will likely water.

I was studying the buck as he was drinking and I realized I was looking at a really good buck. He had long tines, long beams, and a couple of extra points. When you travel as much we do, you have to adjust to seeing huge-bodied Canadian deer one week and much smaller-bodied Southern deer the next. Texas deer generally have smaller bodies and they can fool you because their antlers are more impressive on a small body. Because they have plenty of groceries, Don Montgomery's deer are bigger than most Texas deer.

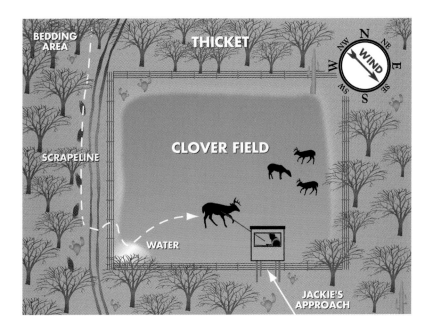

When the deer finished watering, he started toward the other deer in the field. He was about 100 yards from the blind and I decided he was too good to pass up, even on the first day of the hunt. When I sit in a box blind, I always sit on the left side because I'm left-handed and I like to get an elbow rest in the window for my left elbow. This blind worked perfectly for the rest I wanted, and I made an accurate shot. That buck had 167 inches of antler, the best Texas buck I've ever taken.

# TACTICAL BREAKDOWN

Nothing beats hunting on well-managed property where there are lots of big bucks. You'll never shoot a big buck where none exist. During hot weather, water sources become important hunting spots. Our blind overlooked a water source as well as a food plot the deer were using. Though I don't usually shoot a buck on the first day of the hunt, I made a good decision by not allowing this deer to get away.

When you're hunting from a box blind, practice getting a solid rest for your rifle and for your elbow. When the time comes to make the shot, you'll know how to do it. I sometimes cut a piece of $2 \times 4$ and prop it between the front and back window to use as an elbow rest.

## Keys to Success

- If possible, hunt where good bucks exist.
- Hunt around water sources during dry, hot weather.
- Know what quality of buck you're looking for and take him when you get a chance.
- Make sure you have a solid rest for your rifle and your elbow.

# 22

# Drought Buck

Weather conditions often play an important factor in buck quality in a given year. Dry conditions result in fewer groceries for the deer, and they grow poorer racks. Deer are survivors. When forage is scarce, they utilize the food that's available to stay as healthy as possible. When there's plenty of food and the deer's body condition is good, antler growth will max out. When conditions are dry, antler growth suffers, and that's the situation we found near Uvalde, Texas, after a hot, dry summer. South Texas is prone to drought, anyway, but they'd had an especially bad drought that year.

Larry Joe and Marty Moore of Texas Pro Outfitters had planted clover and wheat in a powerline right-of-way that cut through the ranch, and that's where we hunted for three days. We

*Credit: Gene Bidlespacher*

saw a lot of deer activity. It was December and the rut was in full swing. We saw a lot of bucks, and some of them were pretty good, but they just weren't up to the usual standards for that area.

Whenever I'm hunting an area where I may have a long shot, I use a Nikon laser rangefinder to range distant landmarks. I do this as soon as I get to my stand, because I know that when a shooter buck shows up, I may not have time to use the rangefinder on him. You may only have a few seconds to take the shot, and it helps to know about how far the deer is. Our setup on this hunt was perfect for determining distances, because there was a series of power poles running down the right-of-way.

I used the rangefinder to determine distances to power poles out to 300 yards. I was shooting a .300 magnum Remington with Federal 200-grain bullets, and 300 yards was the maximum shot that I was willing to take.

About 8:00 a.m. on the last morning of our hunt, I spotted a pretty good rack moving through the brush. I got my binoculars up and saw it was a shooter. The deer was zigzagging through the brush. He'd come to the edge, then go back in. He was out there about 300 yards, and I was getting ready to take the long shot when a doe came across the right-of-way and disappeared in the brush. The buck took off with her.

I figured we'd never see that buck again, but I was wrong, as that doe walked back out of the brush only five minutes later, and the buck was right behind her. He had his head down, just following the doe. They came out near a telephone pole that I'd ranged at 150 yards. At that range, all I had to do was put the crosshairs right on the buck. I was using a sandbag in

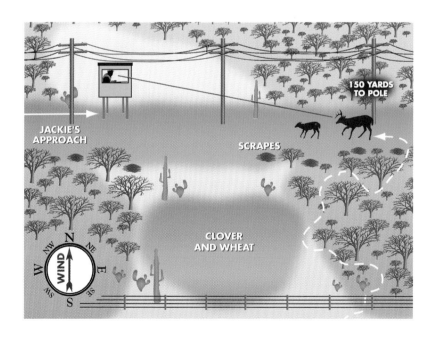

the box blind window for a solid rifle rest and I had my elbow braced against the side of the blind.

I followed the buck in the scope until he stopped broad-side, then I shot. The deer whirled and ran across the right-of-way and into the brush, but he didn't go far. Given the dry conditions, I felt lucky to get a shot at a buck like that. He was a 140-class 10-pointer.

# TACTICAL BREAKDOWN

During a time when natural forage was scarce, we were hunting in a blind where clover and wheat had been planted to attract the deer. There were a lot of deer in the area and the rut was going strong. During the rut, you'll find bucks around concentrations of does. This time of the year, they're not as cautious about coming into open areas in broad daylight.

I used a laser rangefinder to determine the distance to landmarks. That way, I knew about how far the deer was without actually using the rangefinder on him. I can't overemphasize the importance of a solid rifle rest when it comes time to shoot a deer.

## Keys to Success

- Food plots are even more effective when natural forage is scarce.
- During a drought year, you may have to lower your expectations for trophy bucks.
- Where there are logical landmarks, use a laser rangefinder to determine distances before your deer shows up.
- Use a sandbag or any other aid to secure a solid rifle rest.

# 23

# Running 10-Pointer

Sometimes you have to take whatever the deer give you. That happened to me one year when I was hunting in Mexico with outfitter Bill Whitfield. The weather was hot and the deer weren't moving all that well. We mostly hunted from a stand situated on a plateau looking down into a creek drainage. The visibility was excellent. The deer would move along the creek, and they'd also chase does back and forth through the area. It was a good setup.

We got one tremendous deer on video, but the buck was 400 yards away—too far for a shot. We also saw the best 7-point buck I've ever seen. He had a tremendous frame and great mass—everything but a lot of points. I would have shot that deer any day of the week but, again, I didn't have a shot.

*Credit: Gene Bidlespacher*

The last afternoon of our hunt, I was glassing a plateau that must have been 1000 yards away. I spotted a doe bedded down, and two bucks with her. With the sun hitting his antlers, one of the bucks looked good even at that distance. We were running out of time. Our guide, Clay Young, had left us a two-way radio in case we needed to contact him. We could have just gotten out of the blind and gone to the deer, but we only had about 20 minutes of shooting light, so I called Clay on the radio and he came and got us in the truck.

We circled where I'd seen the deer, then we got out and started making a stalk with the wind in our face. We came up over the hill and looked over a small valley, but there were no deer. We knew the deer had to be just beyond the next ridge. We stayed as low as possible and eased up to where we could see over the second ridge, and immediately spotted a doe and a buck, moving from left to right. We had to retreat and circle 300 yards to get a good angle on them.

When we eased back over the edge, I thought we'd be in range but there was still a question of who was going to see who first? An 8-point buck answered that question by bolting out in front of us. I ran up about four or five steps to improve my angle, and immediately saw a doe off to my right. As soon as she moved, a big 10-pointer moved right in behind her.

I don't like to shoot running deer but this was clearly a case where I didn't have a choice. I knew the deer had seen us and would not stop. The deer were moving right to left, gaining speed, and then disappeared into a little patch of brush. I got

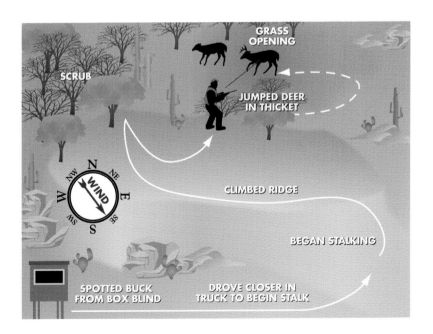

down on my knee as quickly as I could and got on the buck when he came running out of the cover. I swung the crosshairs right past his shoulder as he burst out of the brush, and squeezed the trigger. The buck donkey-kicked and disappeared from sight, but we knew it was a good shot.

That buck scored about 140 and I would not have gotten him if we hadn't been willing to adjust. We kept seeing bucks that were too far to shoot, and finally made up our minds to go after one of them.

# TACTICAL BREAKDOWN

I prefer to hunt from a stand, but sometimes you have to make your own luck. Whitetails are extremely alert and difficult to stalk but it can be done, especially if you spot the deer in the distance and know about where it is.

When you're stalking deer, you must be prepared to make a quick decision to shoot or not to shoot. You must also be prepared to take a shot that's less than ideal. If you're forced to shoot at a running deer, swing slightly ahead of the deer before you shoot and keep swinging to follow through.

## Keys to Success

- Adjust to the situation. If the deer don't come to you, go to them.
- When stalking, move cautiously, keep the wind in your face, and be prepared for a quick shot.
- You must lead a running whitetail and follow through as if shooting a moving target with a shotgun.

# 24

# Hunt Of A Lifetime— Matthew Bowles

For years, Buckmasters has been organizing a deer hunt for disabled kids. It's one of the neatest, most satisfying things we do. When you look up the word "courage" in the dictionary, there ought to be photographs of these kids next to the definition. One year, I got a letter from a little boy in Georgia named Matthew Bowles. Matthew was 11, and he was a real sick little boy. He had cystic fibrosis, and he wrote me that his dream was to take his first buck with Buckmasters.

We got Matthew into our disabled hunt. His mother, Laura, brought him up. Matthew was an instant hit. He had a spark in his eye and his presence just lit up the room. I told our

*Credit: Gene Bidlespacher*

crew that we needed to make sure this kid got a deer. Unfortunately, we had a full moon and the deer hunting was slow. Matthew's mom had to sit with him and keep an oxygen bottle handy while he hunted. We put them in a good stand where they hunted for a couple of days without getting a shot. We finally did a silent drive to make the deer move. A nice buck came by and Matthew made a good shot on the deer. Then a much bigger buck came out, stopped, and just stood there looking at them.

When Matthew got back to the camp, he was so excited telling about his deer. I still get choked up about it. The Buckmasters Classic was coming up and we invited Matthew as our special guest. He got to meet the celebrities, including his hero, Atlanta Braves third baseman Chipper Jones. Chipper hunted the same stand that Matthew had hunted, and Matthew would wait up for him every night to see if Chipper had seen the big buck. Sure enough, Chipper wound up shooting that deer!

During the Classic we got comedian Jim Varney to dress up like a wrestling champion, and we introduced him as such. Then we called Matthew up from the audience to wrestle Jim Varney and, of course, Matthew won. At the Classic Awards Banquet, we created an award called The Mighty Fine Fellow Award and gave it to Matthew. There wasn't a dry eye in the house.

Not long afterwards, Matthew took a turn for the worst. We rushed the taxidermist to finish Matthew's deer mount and shipped it to his parents. His mom told me that she took the mounted deer into Matthew's hospital room. He petted it, felt the horns, and just smiled and smiled. An hour later, he passed away. That experience will stay with me for the rest of my life. We've created the Buckmasters Lifetime Hunt for sick kids whose lifetime dream doesn't have anything to do with an amusement park. Their lifetime dream is to go deer hunting, and we try to make that dream come true for as many kids as we can. We still

give the Mighty Fine Fellow Award at the disabled hunt every year, but now it's the Matthew Bowles Mighty Fine Fellow Award.

# TACTICAL BREAKDOWN

Anytime you have an opportunity to help someone who's less fortunate, you'll probably be the one who benefits the most. Whenever I start to dwell on my personal problems, I just stop for a minute and remember the kids we've had on our disabled hunt.

I especially think about Matthew Bowles and how many lives that brave young boy influenced. Deer hunting can teach a lot of valuable lessons. Some of the most important lessons don't have a lot to do with white-tailed deer.

## Keys to Success

- When hunting with someone who you really want to get a deer, put him in your best stand first—as we did with Matthew.
- Especially if your guest hasn't shot many deer, tell him not to be too choosey. He should shoot the first good buck he sees; a buck doesn't have to be record-class to be a trophy.

# 25

# Late Bow Buck

Luck is a wonderful ally when you're hunting whitetails, but persistence is also valuable. In Montana one fall, we were hunting during the early October bow season when we spotted a good 10-point buck. We hunted that buck for a solid week and never caught up to him. We were confident that we were hunting correctly, and it was just a matter of time before we got a good shot at him.

In Montana, there is a week-long break between bow season and the combined bow/rifle season. We took a break as well and went home to Alabama. We returned to Montana when the rifle season opened and were lucky to find that the deer had not changed their patterns.

*Credit: Gene Bidlespacher*

We were hunting a food source—sugar beets and corn. The deer were bedding a long way from the food source, and we had set up our tree stands near the bedding area. Most hunters concentrate on the food source because it's easy to identify. In fact, they tend to hunt too close to the food source. If the deer have far to travel in the afternoon, they may not reach the food source until dark. And if you hunt too near the food source in the morning, you'll spook deer when you go to the stand.

This particular stand location was a good one. It was in a brushy bottleneck between the bedding area and the feeding fields. Three game trails came within bow range of my stand. We had a northeast wind that day and the deer were bedding to our north, so the setup was ideal. It was a cool afternoon, and we got in the stand about 2:30 p.m.

About 4:00 or 4:30 I saw a buck coming through the thicket, heading east. He was traveling on the trail that was about 30 yards to my right. As he walked along, he suddenly turned and headed directly toward me. I could tell this was the same deer we'd videotaped during bow season. The deer fed as he moved slowly along, and finally turned back onto the main trail.

I try not to draw my bow or move at all if I can see the deer's eye. If I can see the deer's eye, I figure he can see me. If you sit absolutely still, deer may look right at you and not

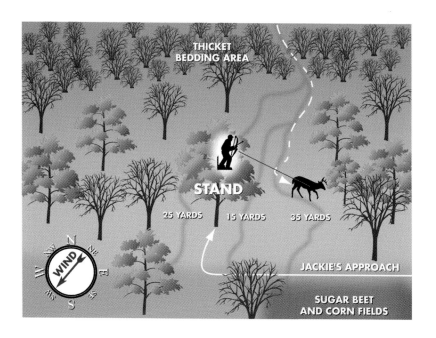

recognize you as a threat. They are very good at noticing movement, however. Even if I'm well camouflaged and high in a tree, the deer may spot my movement. In this case, the buck finally turned his head to the left and I was able to draw and make a good shot on a very nice buck.

# TACTICAL BREAKDOWN

We were successful on this hunt because we did our scouting homework and we were familiar with the deer movements. We've taken a lot of bucks on this setup over the years by getting as close to the bedding area as possible and waiting for a north to northeast wind.

This was another case of scouting to identify the deer's travel pattern, then being confident in our setup and patient enough to wait for a good shot.

## Keys to Success

- Especially when bowhunting, it's critical to let the deer get within shooting range.
- Never draw your bow if you can see the deer's eye. Wait until he moves behind an obstruction before drawing, so he can't see your movement.
- When hunting between bedding and feeding areas, try to set up closer to the bedding areas if possible.

# 26

# Borderline Buck

Weather plays a major role in deer activity. It would be great if you were able to take a vacation from your job and take advantage of perfect hunting weather whenever it occurred, but few deer hunters are that lucky. Most of us wind up hunting on weekends and holidays, regardless of weather.

At Buckmasters, we try to schedule our hunts for the peak periods of the rut, but the hunts are scheduled months in advance and there's no way to predict the weather. We traveled to Pennsylvania, along the Maryland border, for a rifle hunt during the rut. Unfortunately, we came at a time when the weather was very hot, muggy, and foggy. Deer movement had shut down, and our video cameras were having all sorts of problems with the weather.

Credit: Gene Bidlespacher

The deer we saw were leaving the feeding fields before daylight, and were not coming back to the fields until after dark. Rather than fight difficult conditions, we bailed out and returned a week later when the weather conditions were more favorable. The weather was a lot colder by then, and deer activity had picked up considerably.

In this particular setup, we were hunting the deer as they came out of a big clover field and traveled along a huge, very thick hardwood ridge. To reach our morning stand without spooking the deer, we had to circle way down on the back side of

102

the ridge to get the wind right, and then ease in to the tree stand. We were hunting deer as they traveled through the transition area—the hardwood ridge—back to their bedding areas.

If you want to be a successful deer hunter, there are times when it's necessary to get out of bed very early, and this was one of those times. We were in our stand that morning an hour before daylight. A few deer moved right at daylight and then we hit a lull. At 9:00 a.m., I saw some movement in a very thick patch of woods. Using binoculars, I could tell it was two bucks working their way down the ridge. The cover was so thick that I couldn't tell much about the deer other than that they were bucks.

Then I saw two other bucks, and I could tell by the way they acted that they were getting ready to fight. We could hear them thrashing brush and putting on aggression displays, but the cover was so dense that it was difficult to see what was happening. An accurate shot at either one was impossible.

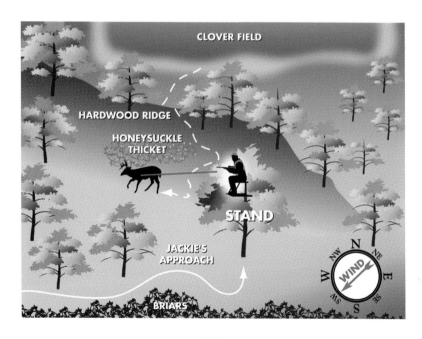

Now two more bucks came down the ridge and bedded down right in front of us. One of the deer had a good rack. I studied him through my binoculars, and I could see that his beams curved around in front of his nose, a good indication of long beams. The buck's back tines were eight to 10 inches long and his brow tines were good. He looked like a shooter, but he was bedded down.

After about an hour, the deer stood up and I could see him rubbing a tree—really tearing it up. I couldn't see his body well enough for a shot, but I could see the tree violently swaying back and forth. About that time, another buck came up and challenged the deer I was watching. They squared off, but it wasn't much of a fight. Once the challenger backed off, the target buck started moving down the ridge. When he got to an opening, I grunted and he stopped broadside at about 75 yards. I made a good shot with my Remington 300 Mag, and under the circumstances, was fortunate to get the deer.

# TACTICAL BREAKDOWN

The deer were moving well and the bucks were aggressive. Our stand was between the feeding field and the bedding area, but the deer surprised us by bedding on the ridge. Luckily, they bedded within 100 yards of our stand location.

We really got lucky when another buck's presence encouraged our target deer to leave his bed and eventually offer a shot.

## Keys to Success

- If deer are moving early, the only way to get on them is to get up super early and get to your stand way before daylight.
- Use a grunt call to make a buck stop in his tracks and offer a shot.

# 27

# Record-Book Buck
# With a Bow

The 10-point buck on the next page was taken with a bow and arrow in the fall of 1988 in south Texas. We had been still-hunting all morning, and were preparing to go back to the truck for lunch.

Before coming out of the stand, I looked over at an oak flat through my binoculars and noticed a rack buck feeding on acorns. It was extremely windy that morning, and I knew I had a chance to move after the buck and not be heard in the crunchy leaves.

There was a ditch-like area with a brushy bottom between me and the oak flat that gave me the opportunity to move within bow range without being spotted.

When I spotted the buck, he was feeding away from me. I got in that ditch and kept the brush between me and the deer until I reached the edge of the oak flat. I had the wind in my face—which was critical. I also had the cover to keep me concealed, so I could pop up and see where the deer was and then go back down and walk. Once I got up to the edge of the oak flat where the deer was feeding on the live oaks, I noticed that it was bottle-necking up in front of me. There was an opening going to another oak flat.

I made sure I kept my eye on the buck the entire time—he was feeding away from me and at an angle. I crawled along the edge to get out in front of him. That way, if he cut through from the one oak flat to the other, I'd still be in position to have a shot. I finally reached the edge, got into good cover, and stayed on my knees. The wind was perfect. He was feeding his way out to the end of the bottleneck and was going to cut across the opening to the next oak flat. When he got out there—this was in the days before the rangefinder—I just used my eyes. Taking a visual measurement—one yard, two yards, three yards, and going from object to object until I got out to the deer—I guesstimated the yardage at 25 or 30 yards. I waited while he was cutting across, hoping he would turn broadside. When he did, I grunted at him and he stopped and looked up. I was at full draw; I let the arrow go and made a good shot. He didn't go 50 or 60 yards.

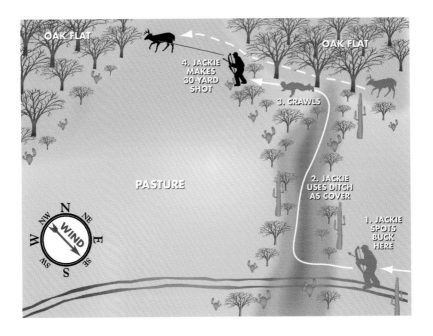

# TACTICAL BREAKDOWN

On this hunt, I was able to spot the deer from a distance with binoculars and use the cover to get to him without him seeing me. I also had the wind to my advantage. There were two sets of cover—a ditch and an oak flat that bottlenecked in the direction he was headed. I noticed an opening to another flat and knew he would take that bottleneck and cut out in the open and go on to the next one.

Still-hunting on the ground with a bow is tough. I kept the cover between me and the buck. I always kept my eye on him and made sure that he wasn't looking back and was feeding away from me. I was fortunate to make a good shot and take my first record-book deer with a bow.

## Keys to Success

- Always inspect your surroundings one last time before coming out of your stand. I did—and it paid off with a record-book buck!
- Use all available cover to your advantage, especially when you have to sneak up on a deer.
- To key noise to a minimum, move when the wind is blowing, stop when it ceases.

# 28

# Fenceline Buck

Scouting is critical to successful whitetail hunting, and early season scouting is no exception. Before the Alabama archery season opened one fall, I spent some time scouting my deer lease, and I liked what I saw. The white oak acorns were really dropping, and that's something I always watch for. Deer like white oak acorns because they have less tannic acid and are not as bitter as other acorns. White oak acorns must seem like candy to a deer.

White oaks don't produce acorns every year, so it really pays to scout the hardwoods and determine which trees have a good acorn crop. During my scouting for this hunt, I used my binoculars to look up into the trees for acorns, and found there was an excellent crop. In fact, some of the acorns had already started to drop.

*Credit: Pat Gregory*

Another important piece of scouting that I did for this October hunt was to walk a nearby fenceline and find where deer were crossing it. Crossings are usually pretty obvious, as deer repeatedly going under a fence will create a depression and kill off the vegetation. I found a huge trail under one section of fence. There was a lot of hair on the barbed wire, so I pulled the hair off and checked it again in two days. There was a lot more hair on the fence the second time I checked it, so I knew the crossing was being used regularly.

The trail under the fence connected with the ridge where the white oaks were dropping acorns. There was a clover field on the next property and a soybean field on a property about a mile away. I figured the deer were feeding in those fields at night and moving back into the woods to feed on acorns before bedding for the day.

From examining the trails, I could tell that the deer were either walking the fenceline on our side, or they were coming from the adjacent property and going under the fence at the big crossing. We set up a tree stand in the biggest white oak on the ridge, in a spot where three trails came together. There were still plenty of leaves on the trees, so the stand was well concealed. With the trails right in front of me, it was an ideal setup.

I got into the stand early that morning. As soon as the sky started to lighten, I saw several does moving through, all feeding on acorns. I felt confident that my plan was a good one.

About an hour later, I caught the glint of antlers coming through the trees. The buck was walking the fenceline on my side of the fence. I just let him come closer until he was in easy bow range. Then I waited until he stepped behind a tree so I

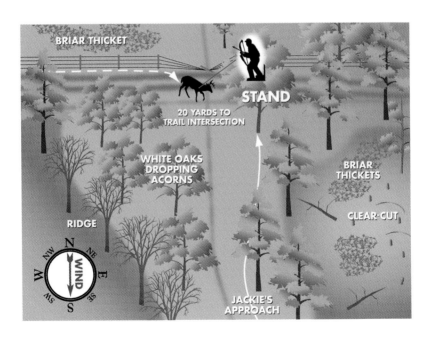

could draw my bow without him seeing the movement. When he reached the intersection of two trails, I grunted softly with my mouth and he stopped to try and pinpoint the sound. That's when I made the shot.

# TACTICAL BREAKDOWN

Preseason scouting paid off with a good buck. I was familiar with the hunting area and I knew what to expect, but it's always a good idea to spend some scouting time on the ground prior to the hunt. The key this time was white oak acorns and active trails that led to the white oak trees.

## Keys to Success

- If deer are following fencelines, look for areas where they cross, and plan your hunting strategy accordingly.
- When bowhunting, wait until a deer moves behind a tree or other obstruction, so you can draw your bow without being detected.

# 29

# The Logo Buck

The hunt that produced the symbol for Buckmasters—we call it the Buckmasters logo buck—is one hunt that is freeze-dried into my memory.

The buck I took on that hunt is the one on our *Buckmasters Whitetail, Rack,* and *Young Bucks Outdoors* magazines; the one that is seen at the opening and closing of the "Buckmasters" TV shows, and in other places, including the Buckmasters stickers on the back windows of our members' trucks around the country.

It was 1987 and Russell Thornberry, the editor of *Buckmasters Whitetail* magazine, had invited me go hunting in Alberta, Canada. Before joining Buckmasters, Russ was an outfitter along the Battle River. We were hunting there in mid-November.

Russ hunted these whitetails by staying on his side of the river, even though the deer were on the other side. Hunters never

crossed the river unless they shot a deer. The setup made sense because it kept human activity in the deer's territory to a minimum.

It was late in the afternoon, and as we were coming up the
hill toward this area, Russ glanced over and said, "Whoa, whoa,
whoa! There's a doe right there." And then this huge buck stepped
out. We hit the ground and rattled and tried to make him react to us,
but nothing happened and it was getting close to dark. Russ said,
"The only chance we've got is to go down and try the tripod."

Our tripod stands with swivel seats were close to the
river, and were set where the wind was in our faces. The woodlots across the river finger down toward the water and bottleneck
to a point. The bucks go from the bottlenecks across an open
pasture to the next woodlot. There was a gap in there of about
200 yards, and these deer would go skirt from one woodlot to another. Our stands were set where we could catch the deer as they
came out of the woods to cross the pasture.

The only thing on my mind while I was in the tree stand
was this huge buck we were trying to rattle. We didn't have any

luck, though, so I said, "We can get on him tomorrow." But 10 minutes later, here came a couple of does out of the bottleneck and into the pasture. A nice buck was behind them.

The deer was kind of trotting—he wasn't running real fast. I decided he was a shooter buck. I put the crosshairs in front of his shoulder. When I shot, the deer stopped and just looked at me. I missed him! I'd just shot right over him. And when he looked at me, I knew what I'd just missed—a major record-book buck.

I quickly jacked in another shell, shot, and he went right down. Russell asked, "Did you get him?" I said, "Yeah, he went down." He said, "Alright, let's go!"

Then he said: "This is going to be the coldest cold you've ever felt." Man, was he right. We had to walk across the river to the deer. The river was 60 to 80 yards across, but the air temperature was −30°F! The water was between ankle and knee-high. It went over the tops of my 10-inch boots, and when it hit my skin—

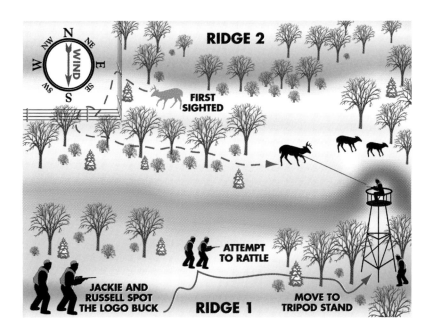

I mean, I've never felt cold like I felt cold that afternoon. I got out on the other side of the river and started running, jogging up and down, back and forth, anything to get my circulation going.

Finally, I looked back at the tree stand and tried to get a point on where this deer was down. I didn't see the buck. I didn't see anything. I knew what I'd shot at and I was getting that sick feeling. But Russ had swung back around and about that time he said, "I think I've found what you're looking for."

I'll never forget it. I walked over there and just blurted out, "Oh, my God." It was a magnificent buck.

The outfitters took a step ladder across the river, put the deer on top of the ladder, then ferried it across.

Buckmasters senior vice president Alan Brewer sat in that stand for three days before I got there and didn't see anything. I sat in it for 10 minutes and got our logo buck.

# TACTICAL BREAKDOWN

The main thing was getting the wind right and catching the deer taking the bottleneck from one woodlot to the next.

But staying out of the area where the deer liked to travel was also a significant part of the success here. Since the only time anyone went across the river to where the deer were was when they shot oner, human scent was kept to a minimum.

## Keys to Success

- We kept the wind in our faces, and had stands set up to overlook areas of known deer activity during the rut.
- I had layers of warm clothing on, so was able to withstand the cold long enough to hunt efficiently and take a steady shot.
- We hunted to the end of shooting light, when the buck was moving.

# 30

# Rattling In a Buck

When conditions are right, rattling for whitetails is the most exciting way to hunt. It's also one of the most satisfying methods of killing a mature buck. The prerut is the best time to rattle because the bucks are aggressive and aren't hooked up with does. Later on in the rut, a buck is not likely to leave an estrus doe to check the sounds of two other bucks fighting.

The day after Christmas, 1984, I'd been scouting my lease in Alabama, and had found a set of big tracks crossing a beaver dam in the back of the property. Upon inspection, I saw that the same deer was coming and going across the dam. I couldn't find any tracks of other deer in the area, and I felt pretty confident this was a good buck. The tracks led from the thickest

woods in the area, across the dam, then into a clover field. The woods definitely looked like the type of secure spot for a mature buck to be bedding. The spot wasn't far from the field, but I didn't expect to see the buck out there during daylight. It was almost time for the rut, so I figured there was a chance that I could pull the buck out of his sanctuary by rattling.

On New Year's Day, we got the wind I needed to hunt that buck, so I slipped into my spot that afternoon and got set up. I put my rattling horns together, but not loudly. I started off just tickling the tines a little bit, and grinding the horns in a way that wouldn't make much noise. Then I grunted a few times with a grunt call and waited. Nothing happened.

Rattling is an unpredictable hunting technique. Sometimes it doesn't work at all even when conditions seem perfect. Other times, when conditions are poor, the deer respond very well. Some bucks come on a run, while others sneak in to the fight. You have to stay alert because you never know when or where a buck will show up.

I waited 30 minutes, then started a second rattling sequence, this one more violent. I made more noise this time, hitting the tines pretty hard and grinding them together like two bucks really getting after it. I stayed with that sequence about 30 seconds, then grunted a few more times and waited.

It took only two or three minutes before I saw something move over on the beaver dam. I could see a deer coming through the cover. Once it cleared, I could tell it was a good buck, and it was walking along the same trail that I'd scouted. The buck moved along cautiously, looking in my direction, curious about what sounded like a fight in his territory. I had my rifle up and watched him come another 20 steps until he reached a clearing where I made the shot.

He was a heckuva buck. He weighed more than 220 pounds live weight, and he was the biggest buck I'd rattled up in Alabama until that time.

# TACTICAL BREAKDOWN

Scouting and being able to read tracks had pinpointed the bedding area of a deer that I felt sure was a mature buck. I consequently set up in a spot that overlooked the major trail the buck was using. Rattling to attract a buck is a technique that fails more often than it succeeds. It's important to know what the deer are doing in your hunting area and when you're likely to attract a buck by rattling. Finally, you must stay alert and have confidence in your hunting plan.

## Keys to Success

- When rattling, always start off quietly, just tickling the tines, then wait maybe 30 minutes. Next time, do it louder, to simulate bucks that are beginning to get worked up.
- Different bucks respond to rattling in different ways. Pay particular attention to the area downwind of your position. Many bucks will come in quietly.

# 31

# Coyote Drive

W hen you're scouting for a bowhunt, you've really got to do your homework. A bowhunter must put himself in position to be within 30 yards of the deer, and that's a lot different than scouting for a firearms hunt, where your effective range is 100 to 300 yards. When I'm scouting for a bow setup, I'm looking for tight cover—some sort of funnel that brings the deer very close to my position.

In Alabama one January, we were doing our usual scouting for scrapes, and we found a spot where three trails came into a hardwood bottleneck. There were scrapes all around and the situation was perfect for archery hunting. We put up a tree stand and waited for a favorable wind direction.

*Credit: Gene Bidlespacher*

We eased into the stand one morning on a northwest wind. The deer were coming to us from the north. First, we had several does walk right under the stand. We saw a few bucks early but they didn't come our way. Later in the morning, we saw a nice buck far to the north of our location. The deer was following one of the trails that converged on our bottleneck. He was traveling along the trail, not in a hurry, when he suddenly turned and looked upwind, back in the direction he'd just come from.

I saw him raise his tail and I knew something was wrong. The wind was in our favor and I knew the buck couldn't smell us, but I had the feeling there was a bobcat or maybe a coyote that was making him nervous. The deer started running right to us from 100 yards away. He was coming pretty quickly, and I saw that there was a coyote behind him. When the buck reached the spot where the trails came together, he took the main trail and came right at us.

That's how I hoped a buck would move through the area, but I didn't want him coming on a dead run. That's an awfully tough shot with a bow. The cover was thick and I didn't have a lot of time to make a decision about the shot. There was one opening about 20 yards in front of us, but I was concerned that the deer would not hear me grunt and might not stop at all.

I had my bow drawn and was aiming at the opening when the deer got there. I grunted at him real loud and he threw on the brakes, allowing me to make a good shot. If the coyote had kept coming, I would have gotten him, too, but the coyote figured something was wrong and decided to look elsewhere for a meal. You sometimes have the deer scouted perfectly and something weird happens to mess you up. I was lucky that morning. You don't often have a coyote driving deer to you.

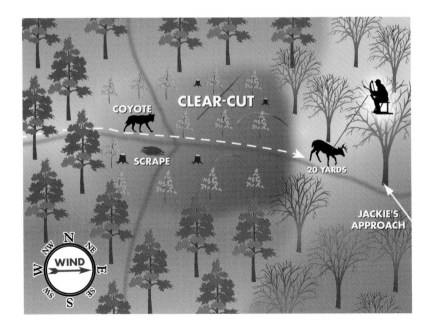

# TACTICAL BREAKDOWN

The approach to a hunting stand is critical. As we did on this occasion, the Buckmasters team gives careful consideration to how we should approach the stand without spooking the deer we think are in the area. If you spook the deer you're hunting, the hunt is over before it starts. With bowhunting, it is critical to set up a stand where deer are funneled within close range.

## Keys to Success

- Always make sure the wind is in your favor. This is especially important in bowhunting.
- Wait for the deer to be in an opening, where you have a shot, before grunting and making him stop.
- If a deer starts behaving abnormally, look for other factors—a coyote, another hunter, whatever. If you're lucky, that "x" factor might drive the deer toward you.

# 32

# 12-Pointer On a Drive

Sometimes the deer just don't move and you have to make something happen. That happened to me in 1994 when I hunted in Idaho with outfitter Tim Craig. The weather was unseasonably warm and the deer were not moving at all. We hunted the entire week with no success. We were down to our last afternoon.

Tim knows his hunting area like the back of his hand, and he knows how the deer use available cover. We decided to set up a silent drive. The idea of a silent drive is to send drivers upwind of a bedding area so their scent drifts through and causes the deer to get nervous. The stand hunter gets situated between the bedding area and the next logical cover for the deer. In a silent

Credit: Gene Bidlespacher

drive, you don't make a lot of noise and you're hoping the deer will try to sneak to the next cover instead of running at full speed.

We were hunting deep draws where a long shot was a distinct possibility. We told the guides to give us about 20 minutes to get into position before they started the drive. We went to a place called Tim's Point, and I found a rock that not only gave me a solid rest (I'm a left-handed shooter), but had the added benefit of breaking up my silhouette.

We'd been in position for only 10 minutes when does started trickling out of the bedding area. In a silent drive, the does are usually the first deer to move. The bucks act more cautiously and let the does go first, in case there's danger downwind. Bucks seem to do more sneaking and looking than running when they're trying to elude a drive.

I saw a slow movement behind the does and spotted a very nice buck, just slipping along. The does had stopped directly below me, just over 200 yards away. It took the buck about five minutes to decide he needed to be down there with the does, but I wasn't able to get a good shot on him. Luckily, he started chasing one of the does, pushing her out into the open where I had a shot.

I had ranged the distance at 220 yards and the angle was very severe, almost straight down. I've missed bucks on downhill shots like that before, and I've learned to aim at the lower one-third of the body to avoid shooting over the deer. That's what I did this time: I put the crosshairs behind the deer's shoulder, in the heart area, and made a solid hit on him. He was a terrific 12-pointer with more than 150 inches of antler.

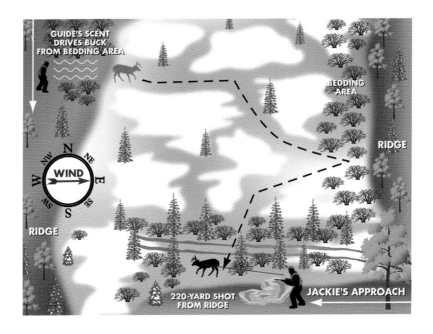

# TACTICAL BREAKDOWN

Knowing how the deer move from one patch of cover to the next is critical when planning a silent drive, as you have to put a stand hunter into position to intercept the deer. Silent drives are good for midday hunting or for situations when the deer just aren't cooperating. Drives work best when you have good visibility and open areas between patches of cover. It helps when the terrain allows you to get above the deer and maintain visibility.

## Keys to Success

- When doing a silent drive, position standers downwind of the cover. Drivers move into the cover from the upwind side, walking silently, making minimal noise to push deer out and not panic them into full flight.
- Use the utmost caution on all drives. Everyone should wear fluorescent orange, and make certain you don't take shots in the areas where other hunters might be.
- Standers should get a solid rest, and try to find a spot where their outline is broken up by cover.

# 33

# Record Buck at −30°F

**W**hen you deer hunt in the Canada, you'd better be prepared for cold weather. On my first bowhunting trip to Saskatchewan, the temperature was −30° to −40°F. Sitting still from daylight to dark in those conditions is tough on an Alabama boy. The hardest thing for me was drawing my bow while wearing all those layers of clothes. But I couldn't sit still without the clothes, so I really didn't have a choice.

I'd done some cold-weather bowhunting before, and I'd learned to lower the draw weight of my compound bow by about five pounds. In Alberta one time, I couldn't get my 65-pound bow drawn to make a shot on a 180-inch buck. I was just too cold to draw the bow. In Saskatchewan, I had the draw weight backed off to 60 pounds.

*Credit: Russell Thornberry*

My outfitter had several stands located around active scrapes in the middle of deep forests. We sat from Monday through Thursday on some good places and didn't have any luck, then moved to a different location when the wind shifted. This new stand had five different scrapes within 20 yards. My camera-man at the time was Pat Gregory, and we used hand signals to tell

each other about deer. Sometimes I saw the deer first and sometimes Pat saw them first. A closed fist meant the deer was a doe.
Index and little fingers up in a "hook 'em horns" sign meant a
small buck. Five fingers up was the sign for a big buck—a shooter.

We got in the stand at 5:00 a.m. and we had a few small
bucks and several does come past but nothing exciting. About 4:00
p.m., I glanced back at Pat and he gave me the five fingers up. I
knew a good deer was coming, but I couldn't see him. The deer
was coming out of the brush, making his way toward the scrapes.

One scrape was about 20 or 30 yards in front of me, but
there were limbs in the way and I couldn't take the shot. The
buck was working toward Pat. The buck finished working his
second scrape and started toward the scrape where I would have
a shot. He had to walk behind one big spruce tree en route to the
third scrape, and I drew my bow when he went behind the tree.

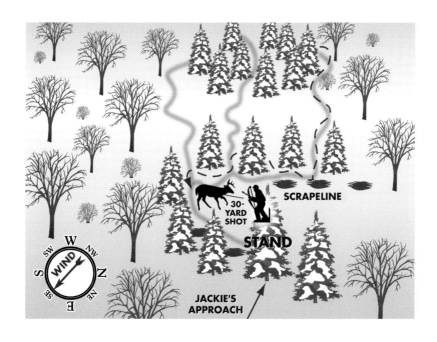

Even with a reduced draw weight, I had trouble drawing the bow with all my clothes and my gloves and then finding the right anchor point for the release. I was fortunate to make a good shot.

That Saskatchewan deer was my first Canadian record-book buck with a bow. He scored 135 points, and we really paid a price for that deer. We sat in bitter cold conditions from before daylight until dark Monday through Friday and got him on the last afternoon.

# TACTICAL BREAKDOWN

Just being able to sit still in bitter-cold temperatures is a major achievement. The key is to dress in layers. Bowhunters should wear an outer layer that is tight enough so as not to restrict their ability to draw the bow. Keep snacks in plastic bags and put them, along with drinking water, inside your clothes, next to your chest. That keeps them from freezing. Whatever you do, don't carry snacks in a paper bag when it's bitterly cold. Opening a frozen paper bag sounds like an earthquake in the woods.

## Keys to Success

- In bitter cold, back off on the draw weight of your bow. Anything to make it a bit easier for you makes sense when the temperatures are well below zero.
- During the rut, you can't go wrong by watching active scrapes.
- Don't go into a stand unless the wind is right; being upwind of fresh scrapes will only alert bucks to your presence.

# 34

# First Saskatchewan Rifle Buck on TV

During the fall of 2000, we hunted in Saskatchewan with Thunderchild Outfitters. I'm always looking for the perfect tree to put a stand in, but that tree doesn't always exist. You have to do the best you can under the circumstances, and that's what happened in Saskatchewan.

We put our stand in a poplar tree between some poplar thickets that were loaded with scrapes and trails. There were no big spruce trees handy in which to put the stand, so we put it in the biggest poplar tree in that area. We were hoping to catch the bucks moving between thickets.

*Credit: Gene Bidlespacher*

We eased into the stand at daybreak and quickly had a nice buck come right past the stand. I didn't think he was big enough, though, so I passed on him. Late in the morning, we saw a big-bodied buck chasing a doe. He was a real heavy 8-pointer, but he never gave me a good shot. He acted like he knew something was up and didn't stick around for long. We saw a few other small bucks during the day and had some does come past the stand. From all the deer activity, we knew the location was good.

By late afternoon, we had does feeding around our stand. Cameraman Gene Bidlespacher and I both had a gut feeling that a buck might appear from the biggest thicket. We had shooting light until a little after 5:00 p.m., and we were running out of time. At 4:45, I saw a big buck step out of the thicket and stop to test the air. I guessed that he had seen some does that had just walked by, and he was checking them out.

The buck came out of the thicket on a fast walk. As always seems to happen to me, he was on the left side of my stand. Since I'm left-handed, it's much easier for me to make a shot on a deer to the right of the stand, but I'm often stuck with the more difficult shot. Here's a tip for deer hunters. When you climb into a stand and there are no deer in sight, practice getting a solid rest for every angle where you're likely to get a shot. When the deer finally shows up, you may only have a few seconds to make a good shot, and you don't want to waste time trying to figure out how to get the best rest.

The temperature was 0°F that day and I was wearing a lot of clothes, making it hard to twist into shooting position. Furthermore, the buck was walking right toward me and I had to wait until he walked behind a tree before I could move into position for the shot. The buck didn't see me move, but the does sure

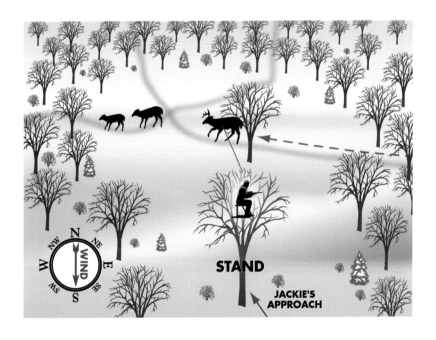

STAND

JACKIE'S
APPROACH

did. They started running, and then the buck started running toward them. I grunted at him and he stopped, giving me a quartering shot. He was a 155-inch buck, and my first Saskatchewan buck taken with a rifle.

# TACTICAL BREAKDOWN

We had a steady north wind, which helped us select a stand where most of the deer would be upwind of our position. A steady breeze is a deer hunter's friend, while variable winds that change unpredictably will get you in trouble. We were hunting during the rut and bucks were pushing does out of the poplar thickets. During the rut, bucks like to chase does in the open, where they can see other bucks moving in on them and where they can keep the does in sight.

## Keys to Success

- When you're in a stand, look for rests and shot angles from all directions *before* a buck shows up. If you wait until he shows up, you probably won't have time to figure out how to position yourself for the shot.
- If you can't find the ideal tree to place a stand in, look for the biggest tree in the area that's still within range of where deer may show up.

# 35

# Late-Morning Buck

If you get a chance to hunt whitetails that have not been pressured, you've got a chance to do something special. Deer that are not hunted hard or have not been hunted in a season tend to be a little more relaxed. We traveled to Montana in October one year, and we were the first bowhunters to hunt this particular area. We'd hunted there several times in previous years, and had stands set up to catch deer moving between planted fields and bedding areas.

This time, the deer were feeding in sugar beets and clover fields. If whitetails know they're being hunted, they don't spend much time in the fields during daylight hours. They leave the fields at daylight and don't return until it's almost dark. We usually scout the trails that deer are using and set up tree stands

*Credit: Gene Bidlespacher*

closer to the bedding areas than the fields. That usually gives us better light for filming and for hunting.

Since we were the first hunters and the deer were feeling no pressure, they were staying in the fields well past daylight every morning. We set up a new stand in an unusually straight cottonwood, near where three trails exited the fields. We were 35 feet up in the tree, but down in a bottom. When deer came off the field, up on a bluff, they were on our level until they walked down into the bottom.

138

The wind had to be perfect for this setup to work. We needed a south or southwest wind in the mornings, a north or northwest wind in the afternoons. We went in the first afternoon with a good wind direction, but the wind shifted on us. The first small buck that came by smelled us right away, so we abandoned the stand rather than risk spooking bigger bucks that we knew were in the area. When you have a tight filming schedule, it's a big deal to give up an afternoon hunt, believe me.

We had a favorable wind the next morning and we got to the stand early. No deer were moving through from the fields at daylight. Using binoculars, I could see deer that were still on the field at 8:00 a.m. Five good bucks came out of the field together. Of the three trails coming through the cottonwoods, two came within bow range of our stand. The other one was 80 yards away, and all five bucks took that trail.

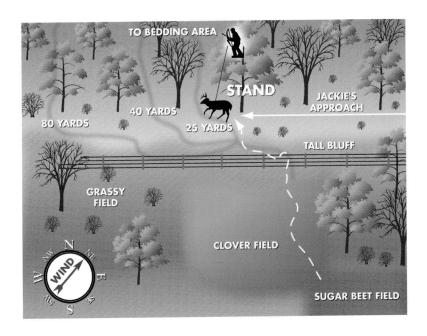

Shortly after 9:00 a.m., I saw three more bucks coming from the field. The cottonwoods still had leaves on them, and that saved us from being detected because I was looking eyeball to eyeball at the deer. When they came to a fork in the trail, two bucks took the 40-yard trail and one took the 25-yard trail. I knew I was about to get a shot.

The buck was on the 25-yard trail, within easy shooting range, when the other two bucks started sparring. The close buck stopped and looked at the other bucks, and that's the chance I was waiting for. I drew while he was looking away, and made an easy shot.

# TACTICAL BREAKDOWN

When the deer are acting in an unexpected manner, you have to adapt your hunting techniques to take advantage. In this case, deer were feeding in the fields unusually late so we relocated our stand closer to the feeding area. We also sacrificed an afternoon hunting period because the wind direction was unfavorable.

## Keys to Success

- Sometimes you have to go much higher in a tree than normal, in order to be above deer coming from high ground.
- Watch the wind. If it shifts, abandon your stand until it's right.
- If there are a number of trails in an area, try to set up so you can cover as many as possible.

# 36

# Broken Nose For a Buck

When you're hunting a specific buck, it can seem as if the deer is outsmarting you at every move. I remember one good buck in Alabama that was not only very frustrating, but which caused me some physical pain as well as emotional distress! It was late in the season and we were hunting two clover fields that were within 300 yards of one another. No matter which field we went to, we'd get a glimpse of our target buck in the other field. The deer was very distinctive and easy to identify. His antlers were very white, and he had lots of points and a wide spread.

The buck outsmarted us, or got lucky, depending on your perspective, on four different occasions. Then we changed our strategy. It seemed as if the deer was sitting back, waiting for us to choose a stand, then intentionally going to the other field. There was an open tree stand on one of the clover fields, while the other field had a stand with a good, solid rifle rest. We finally decided to concentrate on the stand with the good rest and just be prepared to make a 300-yard shot if the buck showed up in the distant field.

I was shooting a 7-mm Magnum that was sighted in to be dead on at 200 yards. I knew the bullet would drop six or seven inches at 300 yards and I practiced a few shots at that range, just to make sure. Then we waited for a day when the wind direction was ideal. We got it one afternoon, just before the season ended.

We got to the stand right after lunch time, and had a few deer come out into the field we were sitting on. If our buck came to that field, we'd have an easy shot. We were also watching four or five does on the other field, however. All of a sudden, a doe came out on the distant field, running low and looking behind her. I scanned the creek crossing and saw antlers back in the woods. Then the buck stepped out and there was no mistaking him, even at that range.

I had already used my laser rangefinder to determine that the far end of the field was 350 yards. The deer was in the middle of the field, about 325 yards from the stand. I waited until he was standing broadside, then got ready for the shot. It was an awkward shooting position for me, as I had to twist around the tree

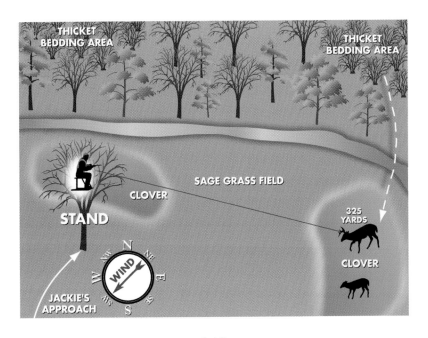

somewhat. I had the rifle up as snug as possible and had as solid a rest as possible, but when I shot, the scope came back and busted my nose. Blood was everywhere! Luckily, the buck went straight down and I didn't have to try a follow-up shot. He was a very good buck, and a deer that I'll remember for a variety of reasons for a long time.

# TACTICAL BREAKDOWN

Persistence paid off, but so did technology and practice. I was shooting a caliber that's known for its flat-shooting trajectory, and I practice shooting at 300 yards. I also used a laser rangefinder to remove all doubt about how far I was shooting. Modern rifles are capable of amazing accuracy, even at long range. Most deer hunters don't practice at distances farther than 100 yards, and they should. They should also use rangefinders so they don't have to estimate distances.

## Keys to Success

- If a deer is constantly fooling, consider the possibility that he has patterned you. Alter your tactics accordingly.
- It really pays to have more than one stand in a given area, even if they are relatively close to each other.
- Try getting to your stand earlier in the afternoon than you normally do. You might not realize it, but it really can make a difference.

# 37

# Alarm Clock Buck

I took the deer shown on the next page on my first hunt with Tim Craig of Boulder Creek Outfitters in the mountains in Idaho.

The deer in this area were feeding in the alfalfa fields at night and coming back to the brushy draws and bottoms to bed up.

Tim and I had seen a big buck the night before and talked about the situation. We decided that I would get down into the brushy draws and catch the deer coming back from the alfalfa. As it turned out, the alarm clock went off late and it was almost daybreak when I got out of bed. I was about 30 minutes behind where I wanted to be.

I also wanted to make sure that my approach would be far enough away from the grain field so that I wouldn't spook the deer. As I was walking along the edge of the cover just before

*Credit: Alan Brewer*

daylight, I caught movement out in the middle of the alfalfa field. That kind of surprised me. I thought the deer would be farther back in the field instead of close to the edge where I was heading. I quickly ducked into nearby cover.

As the light began to break, I used my binoculars and saw a really nice buck—a good 10-point—chasing some does. I had the wind right and I used the rangefinder to range all the way to